DATE DUE

Eating Disorders and Magical Control of the Body

Eating Disorders and Magical Control of the Body is the result of the author's considerable experience of working as an art therapist treating patients suffering from anorexia nervosa and bulimia nervosa. In the course of her work certain themes became apparent, with regard to the content of the patients' art and their associations to it. In particular, numerous images were portrayed of a person, or an animal, eating another, and the theme of being potentially 'swallowed up' in a relationship was widespread.

The book opens with an examination of the concept of magical thinking and its relationship to the wider concept of magic. This type of thinking is then linked to ideas about eating in a variety of settings and cultures and considered in terms of these patients' desperate attempts to be in ultimate, magical, control of their own bodies. Why this should be necessary, what fears they experience in relation to their own bodies and those of other people, is sensitively explored through case histories and illustrations. The last four chapters of the book explore ideas around art, psychic cannibalism and art therapy, and the different ways of approaching the difficulties inherent in working with patients with eating disorders.

Eating Disorders and Magical Control of the Body has a predominantly psychoanalytic perspective, but also draws from areas of mythology, anthropology, religion and literature. It will be of interest to all those concerned with patients or clients who have troubled relationships, both with others and with their own bodies.

Mary Levens is a psychodrama psychotherapist and art therapist at Atkinson Morley's Hospital, London and a staff trainer and supervisor in private practice.

Eating Disorders and Magical Control of the Body

Treatment through Art Therapy

Mary Levens

London and New York

First published 1995
by Routledge
11 New Fetter Lane, London EC4P 4EE

Simultaneously published in the USA and Canada
by Routledge
29 West 35th Street, New York, NY 10001

© 1995 Mary Levens

Typeset in Times by
J&L Composition Ltd, Filey, North Yorkshire
Printed and bound in Great Britain by
Biddles Ltd, Guildford and King's Lynn

British Library Cataloguing in Publication Data

A catalogue record for this book is available from the British Library

Library of Congress Cataloguing in Publication Data

A catalogue record for this book has been requested

ISBN   0–415–12216–3 (hbk)
ISBN   0–415–12217–1 (pbk)

Contents

Introduction

I wanted to write this book after working for a number of years as an art therapist in a psychiatric inpatient unit specializing in the treatment of patients suffering from the eating disorders anorexia nervosa and bulimia nervosa. During this time I have observed a recurring theme either in the content of paintings made by the patients or through their associations with their artwork.

The term 'eating disorders' refers to a collection of symptoms and feelings which relate to eating behaviour, weight, feeling about one's body and food itself. There has been much debate as to whether anorexia and bulimia constitute two separate conditions or whether they are in fact interrelated. However, there are certain specific features which are peculiar to whichever condition predominates. In anorexia, for instance, either severe restriction of food intake or repeated purging or vomiting leads to a marked loss of weight.

Most of the literature refers to women, rather than men, suffering from eating disorders, because aproximately 90 per cent of anorectics are female. The age of onset is commonly between 12 and 23 years. For the diagnosis of anorexia nervosa to be made, a woman must have reduced her body weight by at least 25 per cent and have become amenorrhoeic (stopped menstruating). She must also have begun to experience a morbid fear of becoming fat. The patient herself rarely complains of anorexia because the condition serves an essential function for her. Many bulimic patients, on the other hand, experience extreme distress because they are aware of their loss of control. I am hopeful that, throughout this book, the essential function that both of these symptoms serve for the sufferers, often at an unconscious level, will become apparent.

Despite starvation and an obsessive preoccupation with food, the patient's need to defy a natural relationship with food and to engage in an ongoing tortuous battle with her own body outweighs any other logic. Having worked with these patients for very many years, I cannot emphasize enough the torment that is suffered. These conditions do not emerge solely in the presence of food; they are intrinsically about the woman's experience of her own body and self, with the result that her whole experience is coloured, or rather overshadowed, by a harrowing relationship with herself.

The physical appearance of anorectics communicates clearly to the outside world that something is seriously amiss. The bulimic patient, however, tends to have a normal body weight (although there is a sub-group of obese bulimic patients). These normal-weight women nevertheless have lost control of their eating patterns. When bulimia exists without anorectic pathology, it involves the sufferer in recurrent episodes of binge eating, often involving very large amounts of high-calorie foods which are consumed in secret in a short space of time. This can result in overwhelming feelings of guilt and self-disgust, which are merely exacerbated by the vomiting or purging that follows.

Bulimic women are generally slightly older than anorectics on presentation (around 25 years) and a significant proportion suffer from a range of other 'impulse disorders', which are dynamically linked to the lack of control that is experienced in relation to food. These related behaviours may include substance abuse (e.g. drugs or alcohol), repeated self-mutilation, frequent overdoses, regular shop-lifting, or loss of control regarding sexual behaviour. However, these are descriptions of overt behaviours. What is important for our purpose is the sense of the inner world experience for these women. It is through understanding this that we can begin to make some coherent sense of how these disorders may come about and how they are so fiercely maintained against much opposition. From the outsider's point of view, the life experience of the patient with an eating disorder could be much improved by small adjustments in behaviour. This leads us on to the central questions. What is so vitally important about weight and shape? How can the relationship to food be so grossly distorted that the sufferer is quite unable to recognize, let alone satisfy, hunger or to enjoy the pleasures of good food? Why does the patient dwell in a world where the mere existence of food is experienced as persecutory, as an ever-present monster which is ready to devour her immediately she dares to allow herself to want to eat it?

The purpose of this book is not to explore the differences between anorexia and bulimia but rather to focus on some specific underlying dynamic features which may affect either condition. Throughout the book, therefore, I may refer to either one of the conditions on different occasions, not only because a number of sufferers fulfil the diagnostic criteria for both, either simultaneously or consecutively, but also because the issues of magical perception, the need to control food and the body and the psychological thought processes which I refer to as 'psychic cannibalism' can be found, I would suggest, in both conditions.

The concept of psychic cannibalism was developed in Freud's *Totem and Taboo* (1960), in which he described the belief that incorporating parts of a person's body through the act of eating will lead to the acquisition of that person's qualities. Psychoanalytic theory has linked this concept to the earliest modes of identification. This implies that cannibalistic thoughts or beliefs are inherently bound up with issues concerning not only relatedness but also difficulties regarding separateness, autonomy and individual identity, which are especially pertinent to patients with eating disorders. It has been my experience that cannibalistic fears and fantasies are demonstrated in the clinical setting and therefore may be tackled through the medium of art therapy, which aids the exploration of the relationship between art and magical ideas. The art therapy process is particularly helpful for patients for whom magical ideas predominate.

The early chapters of this book focus on the attempts by patients with eating disorders to control their bodies magically and on the numerous means employed by them to create a more secure sense of self. The discussion covers the notion of 'magical thinking', a term which was refined by the psychologist Jean Piaget in the late 1920s and which refers to a particular style of thinking which occurs in normal development but may predominate in certain psychological disorders. Thereafter the book examines the concept of magic, the psychic development of the human infant, and ideas about the body, particularly from the perspective of the patient with an eating disorder.

The relevance of the boundary of the body is emphasized and this leads to a discussion about what occurs at the interface between two people, that is, two bodies meeting. How can the development of a relationship with another person so strongly threaten the very integrity of an individual's identity? How does this threat come to be experienced concretely in terms of the potential annihilation of the individual's actual existence?

This book examines the nature of the perceived threat to the patient's existence. This threat is both activated and defended against in the patient's relationship to food and in her relationship with her own body. In other words, food and the body appear to be both the source of the threat and the means by which the patient protects herself against the threat. What is the nature of these women's experience of having something inside their bodies which was previously outside? What does food represent? How does food come to threaten so severely their fragile sense of control over their own identity? This concern has fundamental implications for the individual's capacity to relate to another person.

My particular interest in the use of art therapy with these patients lies in the area of creating a channel for communication and in developing a relationship with them. These patients are attempting to maintain a sense of self which cannot be destroyed through intimacy. To them, the source of nourishment that is available to the healthier person from emotional connectedness with another person is the greatest threat to their existence. They are therefore starving in all senses of the word and yet are unable to accept a 'plate of good food' when it is offered in the context of a therapeutic relationship.

How can the therapist engage a patient in the process of taking something good into herself in terms of a nourishing relationship, which will improve her capacity to care for herself in every aspect of life? How can this be achieved without resorting to a form of force-feeding or without merely offering the good food on a plate for the patient to eat eventually when she becomes hungry enough, only to find that the food has gone rotten or that the patient has poured bleach over it?

Art therapy offers an alternative route towards these patients developing the capacity to relate to another person in a healthy way. One of their predominant fears, which is experienced unconsciously, is of destroying the very thing that they are seeking (biting the hand that feeds them) through a seemingly unending torrent of disguised rage at not being in full control of their own needs and wishes. This destructive drive very often leads to a patient's discharge from hospital when she is intent on sabotaging her treatment and yet simultaneously begging to be helped. Art therapy offers an important means of facilitating the expression of these powerful feelings in a contained way. If these feelings are then understood, this enables the treatment to continue.

For those readers unfamiliar with the use of art therapy, a brief introduction will suffice. Thoughts and feelings which are derived from the unconscious often achieve expression in images rather than words. Art therapy enables such images to become an alternative language, perhaps when words are too restrictive or, as is very common, when they are used defensively by an articulate patient. Words can actually get in the way of the true experience of communication. Art therapy allows for both a verbal and a non-verbal means of exploration. The therapist explores with the patient elements of the patient's artwork, such as the use of colour, space and form, and particularly the patient's associations with the images that she has created. Thoughts and feelings which occurred whilst the work was under way are examined, as well as those which arise in response to the completed picture.

All of this happens within the context of a relationship with the art therapist who encourages the patient to explore the whole creative process. The anorectic, for example, frequently panics at being faced with a sheet of empty paper and is unable to make a start without direction. The bulimic commonly expresses a fear of not having enough space. The way in which the patient relates to and uses her paper and art materials is used to explore how she deals with issues such as territory, control and boundaries, and how these issues in turn can help her to understand something about her relationship with her own body and with other people.

Although my primary perspective in this book is psychoanalytic, the fields of anthropology, mythology, religion and literature provide examples when these best seem to illuminate certain ideas. Any human phenomenon should be explored from a variety of perspectives and so I am not seeking to construct only a psychoanalytic interpretation of these concepts and ideas. One of the fundamental distortions of the thinking of the patients with eating disorders whom I shall be describing is holding the belief that only one version of reality is possible, that if differing views are presented simultaneously, then one has to defeat the other. A variety of perspectives will be discussed which will enable different views to be held in mind.

Chapter 1

Introduction to magic

Magic is a vast subject in its own right. I shall be selecting from this field only those concepts which have influenced our past and present modes of thinking and behaving and which have affected the ideas of both society as a whole (our culture) and individuals. I will not be examining the social and political implications of magic.

How does magic enter into the field of eating disorders? The linking concept is that of 'magical thinking'. However, it is important to distinguish between magical ideas as they exist within various cultures and the type of magical thinking on which I shall be concentrating as part of the pathological defences of patients with eating disorders.

My understanding of this distinction lies in the function of magic. Evans-Pritchard, a British anthropologist of the 1930s, considered magic to be an important institution in some societies. The magical belief systems operate to enhance the overall functioning of the group or society and they can actually serve to reinforce essential functions such as social and economic processes within these societies. The function or role of magic therefore depends upon the structure of the society in which it is maintained. This 'social magic' stands in direct contrast to the magical thinking employed by patients with eating disorders, which serves no such social function. Their magic results from desperation. Their magic is one which they feel is the only effective means of surviving, and is aimed at retaining a sense of self which may often imply a magical disconnection from their own bodies. Rather than helping them to become more integrated into their social group, their magic results in their becoming more and more isolated from their own families and social network.

Thus, the magical ideas employed by patients with eating

disorders serve no useful social function. However, because these patients feel that these ideas are all that they have left, the magical thinking acts as a means by which, isolated from their own social group, they can strive to maintain some sense of self and thereby defer or prevent the acceptance of their own bodies. The patient with an eating disorder feels that reduced body mass and content equates with reduced experience of having a body and feelings. Examples of this magical thinking can be seen in her artwork, where she believes that images of secure boundaries around self-portraits will effect greater security. With relation to food, obsessional defences against contact with calories enables her to believe that this will protect her from an ever-possible invasion by (life-embodied) foodstuffs. The magic to which the patient with a severe eating disorder resorts is indeed a means of attempting at all costs to avoid the slow, arduous process of growth. For some it involves a painful wrench away from the primitive and familiar way of existing.

If we were suddenly to find the ability to control the world by the wave of a magic wand – to find that all of our needs could be instantly met without the need to wait in anxious anticipation; that our most desired wishes might be granted; that we were protected from the loved person who might suddenly turn on us, thereby wiping out all that we had once relied upon – then surely we would, with the greatest reluctance, hand over our wand in exchange for an assurance that a healthier person has no need to control his/her environment in such a way; that the potential benefits of living in the real world (which of course demands that we tolerate frustration, disappointment and pain) truly do outweigh magical control.

If we have been lucky enough to discover the benefits of a healthy adaptation to reality, so that there is no need to construct an alternative world to live in which is defined by our own rules of reality, then it may seem to us illogical to imagine opting for the 'quick fix'. After all, we accept that living a life dominated by instant gratification, by finding ways to reduce discomfort immediately, leads to a withering of our mental muscles. It leads, in other words, to a lack of development of our capacity ever to bear the anxieties of life (our responses to external difficulties), with the result that we will be constantly on the run from them, whether through abusing a substance or withdrawing from the external world. Watching videos or compulsively playing computer games may contain some of the same elements of escape from reality that is achieved by heroin or alcohol abuse. As yet it is not so apparent how the abuse of food or of the body serves the same function. Links can be made between the various ways in which human beings attempt to construct their own reality inside in order to protect themselves against the most primitive experience of dissolution. This is the form of magical control which is based on desperate attempts of omnipotence and which leaves the individual highly vulnerable to all forms of collapse.

We can question whether any belief system or practice acts to enhance or to destroy its object. Perhaps, more correctly, we might ask what use an individual or a group makes of any given process? Even psychoanalysis may be questioned in this way. Whereas one person may use the potential experience offered by a certain structure in a way that allows some shift away from a previously more defined, pathological system, another person or the same person at another time may use that opportunity to lend power to his/her destructive wishes, thereby letting go of all brakes and speeding rapidly towards inevitable chaos.

At this stage it might be helpful to look at the way in which magic and magical thinking are explored in the psychoanalytic literature. Rycroft (1968) defines magic as:

> Primitive, superstitious practices based on the assumption that natural processes can be affected by actions which influence or propitiate supernatural agencies or, as in the case of sympathetic magic, by actions which resemble those which the magician wishes to induce.
>
> (Rycroft 1968)

Freud (1960) said that magic must subject natural phenomena to the human will. This definition contains within it one of the core conflicts of patients with severe eating disorders who subject their bodies to the will of their minds. These patients must have absolute control over natural bodily processes. Since they have not achieved a completely integrated sense of their body and mind, they become excessively dependent upon some external regulator to compensate for what is experienced as a state of internal deficiency. Emotional deprivation which was experienced at an earlier stage may be translated by the anorectic, for example, into active deprivation of herself. Rather than being a passive victim, this time at least she feels in control. The bulimic via the symbolic equation of food and nurturing, attempts to supply for herself what was missing.

Freud described the infant's need to use magical thinking as a way of satisfying wishes, at first in an hallucinatory manner. He claimed that belief in the omnipotence of thought underlies all magical ideas and that magical acts are performed in response to specific motives. By making the distinction between primary and secondary processes in thinking we can begin to understand some fundamental links for the patient with an eating disorder. Primary process thinking arises from the desire to satisfy urges and drives and is not bound by logic, by temporal and spatial concepts or even by verbal representations. This aspect of thinking, which occurs in the unconscious, tends to be pictorial and not symbolic. In later stages of development, as secondary process thinking develops, the psychological drive shifts away from the motives of the act to the act itself. This helps us to understand the way in which the 'magical act' is carried out. For example, the act of vomiting in itself begins, after some time, to carry far more significance than purely emptying the stomach of unwanted food. This shift results in an idea which is often held by these patients, namely that an act in itself somehow determines the result in a magical way. Krueger (1989) describes this process: 'incorporating symbolism and magical thinking [was] summarized by a patient who said, "It's like I have anything and everything I've always wanted when I'm in the middle of a binge" '.

Freud was an important contributor to the much criticized but now established belief in the link between the principle of omnipotence in thoughts and the animistic mode of thinking. He compared primitive humans' magical thinking with the logic of schizophrenics and concluded that the same form of thought, in which there is no clear distinction between what is specific to the ego and what is foreign to it, was to be found in children and in other disturbed adults. This has led to debate about the mental functioning of 'primitive' humans being based upon similar principles to those governing the earliest, most 'primitive' stages of child development in western, non-tribal societies. This is a highly complex area. At issue is not so much the question of the universality of human psychological development but rather the meaning which may be attributed to the way in which any group or individual functions. In the minds of many people, there is an association between primitive humans' belief in the power of their wishes and the psychoneuroses of modern humans.

Although many of us today might propose that magical beliefs, shamanism or spells have been replaced by ideas more conducive to a western, post-industrial, scientific society (for instance, in the realms of physics, medicine or psychoanalysis), there are countless examples of ways in which magical beliefs still dominate areas of society (e.g. religion) and individuals within that society.

Another significant writer on the place of magic in the psychological development of the human infant is Jean Piaget. In his book, *The Child's Conception of the World* (1929), he refers to a concept called 'participation'. This implies a relationship between two things or two people, that are partially identical or have direct influence upon each other even when there is no spatial or intelligible causal connection between the two.

Participation is the key feature of magical thinking, that is, of the ways in which people attempt to modify reality. This type of thinking has been described as 'pre-conscious pictorial thought' and involves an equation of the object itself with its representative (i.e. in an idea or an image). Thus, what happens to one will happen to the other. In magical practices it is believed that affecting an external object which is identified with a person causes that person to be affected too.

Magic relates closely to symbolic function. Symbols within magical ideas appear to be participatory and for this reason magical thinking is viewed as utilizing a pre-symbolic mode of thought. Piaget describes the evolution of magical ideas as following a certain law in which

> Signs begin by being part of things, or suggested by the presence of things in the manner of simple conditioned reflexes. Later they end by becoming detached from things and disengaged from them by the exercise of intelligence . . . between the point of origin and that of arrival, there is a period during which the sign adheres to the things although already potentially detached from them.
>
> (Piaget 1929)

Thus, certain behaviours may originally contain no magical element but merely be simple acts of protection. However, with repetition, these acts lose their rationale and become a ritual which in itself performs the desired function. The actions become the cause as well as the sign or symbol. For example, the infant's cry may lead to some action on the part of the mother. A continuity is created between her activity and that of the baby's. The more the environment responds to the baby, the greater his/her sense of participation. Similarly, the discovery by the baby that his/her limbs can move at will may imply that he/she can command the world.

Piaget's contribution to magical thinking is of great importance. He summarizes the magical practices of children as: (a) occurring through the participation of actions and things (where action influences an event); (b) occurring between thought and things (where reality is influenced by thought); (c) occurring between objects themselves (two things must not touch each other); (d) occurring through the participation of purpose. In other words, objects are regarded as living and purposeful, that is, animistic. According to Piaget, if a child believes that the sun chooses to follow him/her around, this belief is animistic; however, if the child thinks that it is he/she who can make the sun move, this idea is founded upon magic and participation.

Freud stated that the animistic mode of thinking, the principle of omnipotence of thoughts, governed magical ideas. It was this that led him to associate these ideas with the internal world of primitive humans, for which he has been sharply criticized. Freud believed that primitive humans (likewise neurotics) had immense belief in the power of their thoughts. Piaget opposed this, distinguishing between the participation and magic of primitive humans and that of both the neurotic and the child.

Freud considered magic to precede animism. In *Totem and Taboo*, he differentiated between the two by suggesting that, whereas magic reserves omnipotence solely for thoughts, animism hands over some degree of it to spirits, and so prepares the way for the construction of religion. How these concepts affect normal human behaviour is more fully understood when considering their presence in everyday thought. Piaget examined ways in which the boundary between the self and the external world may become blurred, for instance in the case of a listener feeling the need to clear his/her throat when hearing the speaker's husky voice. One could find numerous examples, particularly in states of day-dreaming, anxiety or fear. At times of great stress, the attempt to maintain or grasp reality may itself induce some magical thinking or ideas.

For Piaget, animism, as distinct from magic, was the product of participation which a child would feel to exist between the child and his/her parents. Through being unable to distinguish psychical from physical, every physical phenomenon appears to the child to be endowed with will. The distinction between thought and the external world is therefore seen to evolve gradually. The projection of mental relationships into external objects is experienced as concrete and real.

I initially encountered animism in one of the first patients I worked with who suffered from an eating disorder. The 28-year old woman had collected dolls over a number of years. She now had over two hundred and she attributed to each one specific personality characteristics. She would respond to her dolls quite concretely, rewarding them as appropriate. One doll had the power to make her eat (against her will). Only by setting fire to this doll could she prevent its powerful influence. This was a clear example of how behaviour can be related to magical ideas.

The theories of Freud and Piaget offer complementary ideas from psychoanalytic thought and developmental psychology regarding magical thinking. Whereas Freud's psychoanalytic theory of development describes the special affective condition underlying magical beliefs as resulting from narcissism, Piaget thought that this state resulted from an absence of any consciousness of the self. Freud describes the child at this stage as being solely interested in him/herself, in his/her own desires and thoughts which seem charged with a special value. In Piaget's view, if the infant believes in the all-powerfulness of thought, he/she cannot therefore distinguish his/her thought from that of others or his/her self from the external world.

Religion, like art, utilizes the mechanisms of Freud's primary process thought to give structure to abstract concepts. The use of concrete thought is very often culturally sanctioned. Many early religions tended towards the mechanisms of concretization. Within Judaism one can trace a gradual move from paganism to monotheism, which was then adapted by the rest of the world and which involved progressive shifts away from concretization. Indeed, the western tradition of magic is also linked historically to Jewish influences. Although private, personal magic is condemned in the Old Testament, authorized magic was frequently worked by the prophets such as Moses parting the Red Sea. A simple example of the concretization of the expulsion of evil is provided by the ritual in which the sins of the whole community were heaped upon the head of a goat, which was then cast out on the Day of Atonement.

The dual nature of people's attitude toward magical practice and belief is equally well represented by the Old Testament. Jewish magic (actually a combination of Mesopotamian, Egyptian and Greek elements) had a wide reputation in the ancient world, as portrayed by King Solomon who owned a magic ring and understood the language of the animals and birds. On the other hand, Isaiah condemned the mediums and wizards who chirped and muttered.

A number of authors have compared and contrasted the anorectic and the saint. This is a fascinating concept and contains the seeds of much of what will be discussed later. Selvini Palazzoli (1974) declares that the asceticism of the anorectic should not be confused with that of the religious:

> the saint becomes ascetic not as an end in itself but as a means to attain mystical communion with God. . . . Anorectics do not become ascetics after a slow and arduous process of inner development.
>
> (Selvini Palazzoli 1974)

Magical thinking may be demonstrated by describing a bulimic patient in a particular art therapy session. This patient started painting in a state of heightened stimulation. She explained that she had just had a telephone conversation with her mother, during which she had felt punished for deciding not to visit her mother the following weekend. Before painting, she had asked with some emotion, 'How can I ever lead my own life if she constantly makes me feel so guilty for it?' I suggested that she put some of these feelings on to paper. After sitting rigidly for a few minutes, she chose the largest sheet of paper available and then, rather than squeezing the paint from the bottles on to palettes, she gathered up as many bottles as she could in her arms and began frantically pouring the paint directly on to the paper. After watching this for some time, I intervened. 'You've been expressing how this makes you feel. Now how about making an actual picture, using parts of what has come out already?' She went on to cut out parts of the thick mess and to stick these on to another piece of paper. She then began to paint an image of one person inside another.

Expressing her rage, through the pouring of the paints, brought this patient near to tears. The sadness was connected to her associations not only with bingeing in this state but also with the unbearable experience of feeling so enraged with the very person upon whom she felt dependent, a position forcing her to recognize her separateness. The furious merging of all of the colours seemed to me to be a frantic attempt to deny this separateness, to achieve union and to satisfy 'all that she had ever wanted'. The question of whether to spend the weekend at her mother's home or to 'lead her own life' mirrored her true struggle and the punishment that she felt for choosing to 'reject' her mother served to create a conflict which made it yet more difficult for her to 'leave home'. The initial use of the materials was in effect a magical attempt at control. The materials became endowed with a life of their own. The painting takes on a transitional quality as the different materials are experienced in an animated form. This process also occurs for the patient with an eating disorder in her relationship to food.

I have seen numerous paintings made by patients with eating disorders in which they, or some substitute which they recognize to be a symbol of themselves, are sitting on mountain tops, on coulds or in heaven and are looking down at earthlings. The paintings, which are complemented by fantasies of omnipotence, ultimate control and ensured safety illustrate the position of the all-seeing untouchable, unreachable disembodied spirit (see Figure 1.1).

Figure 1.1

This god-like posture performs an important function in the relationship that these patients have with their own bodies. For the anorectic, the counting of calories may itself create the required safety and security. The action develops into a magical means of protection, in that the symbol remains attached to what it represents. The symbol of the skeletal body becomes attached to such concepts as helplessness and demarcation from others. To change (i.e. to give up) this 'frame', the anorectic is giving up not simply a symbol for the self but the *actual* self.

The individual with an eating disorder cannot bear the limitations imposed upon her external reality, in other words, the challenge to her omnipotence; something which is not easily relinquished in normal development. Giving up magical control presents the patient with a vast challenge to her way of thinking. There is commonly a distorted sense of time. It is rather as if one were experiencing great physical pain and the idea of having to wait for a period of time until it passed was overwhelmed by the immediacy of the experience and so time lost its meaning. The psychological pain suffered by these patients demands any immediate action that can promise relief. Such action may comprise a variety of impulsive forms of behaviour: alcohol, drugs, self-mutilation, sexual activity, and of course bingeing or vomiting. Even abstaining from food demands an active will; food refusal is not a passive giving up of eating, it is a highly concentrated activity.

In questioning the social function of any given behaviour, as many feminist writers have done with regard to eating disorders, we could look at the relationship between women's requirements of their own bodies and the various images portraying how women's bodies should appear. Social and political ideologies idealize certain images of femininity for a range of complex economic purposes which are intricately related to power. This is an important subject in its own right, which cannot be properly dealt with here. Suffice it to say that it would be hard to argue the point that contrary to the supposed idealized image of the 'slim' or 'attractive' female, the emaciated anorectic actually becomes increasingly isolated and anti-social in her behaviour as the illness progresses. At first she refuses only to eat with others, but in the chronic stages she isolates herself from much social contact because her internal reality, which is dominated by her own private and peculiar concerns, often cannot be combined with normal social interaction. I have encountered many desperately lonely anorectics, who maintain that they have to live apart from ordinary human interaction because the obsession with food and their own bodies gradually takes over their internal world. Any social interaction then becomes merely an interruption to their own preoccupations. Paradoxically, the more expansive these ruminations are, the more the world of the severely disturbed anorectic is reduced eventually to the size of one calorie.

It will have become apparent by now that the type of disturbance I am describing is of a very serious nature. The underlying personality structure of the patients exhibiting such thinking could be called borderline or actually psychotic in the sense that the principles which govern their mental functioning, the way in which thoughts are constructed and the type of defences which are utilized are of a primitive nature. This means that the unwanted symptoms are needed not only because they serve some unconsciously useful function but also because they act as a life-preserver in the same way that a life raft would be grasped by a person in danger of drowning. Thus, when we suggest to a patient that she give up her symptoms, we are asking her to do something which she perceives as extremely dangerous.

As highlighted by Freud, primary process thinking depends upon the existence of an object rather than upon a mental representation of it. This deficiency in the process of symbolization is an extremely important aspect of the mental functioning of people who resort to using substances of some kind to alter their mental state. It is as if, for them, there is a distinct lack of trust in ideas and words which can evaporate. Only the actual 'concrete' presence of the required object, whether that be a particular person or substance, is felt to be valid. I have heard many anorectics describe how the only sensation that gives them a sense of being real is when they become sufficiently emaciated to be able to feel their bones pushing through their skin.

For individuals hampered by the lack of symbolic capacity in their thinking, thought and action are easily mixed. This is a significant feature in many patients who lack control over their impulses or in patients who 'act out', who lack the symbolic space which would otherwise help them to separate a thought from the need to put it immediately into action. It is this difficulty in thinking that often propels someone towards a binge, a drink or a fight. The perception and experience of, for example, emptiness, loneliness or rage cannot be contained as a thought. Both the intense desire for immediate discharge of the discomfort through action and the limited conceptual capacity to realize the very possibility of experiencing discomforting thoughts or feelings without having to express them in action lead to behaviour which duly reinforces the belief that nothing else would have been possible. For these patients, therefore, having an aggressive thought towards a loved person carries with it the danger of actually damaging that needed person.

Given that there are different types and uses of magic, both societal/cultural and individual, which may be used for the benefit of a group or for the rescue of an individual, how does this relate to the treatment of patients with eating disorders? Fenichel, a psychoanalyst in the 1940s, stated:

> The influence of magic is greater in medicine than in pure natural science, due to the tradition of medicine which stems from the activities of the medicine man and priests. Within medicine, psychiatry is not only the youngest branch of this magic-imbued science but also the one most tainted with magic.
>
> (Fenichel 1946)

In fact, psychoanalysis may be said to have developed from hypnosis which in turn emerged from mesmerism, a form of mental healing. Of course, the healing power of Lourdes or of a Catholic confessional still retains great importance in our society. Thus, on the one hand, we have the magic inherent in part of our approach to and understanding of mental illness and, on the other hand, the magic of the sick person. We cannot help but apply value-laden concepts to try to make sense of these different forms of thinking. However, as professionals, it is worth checking how we too make use of our own 'magic' and for what purposes.

So far, we have seen that certain links do exist between the magical ideas held by patients with eating disorders and the magical ideas of certain culturally sanctioned beliefs. Any distinction between the ideas is not so much in their content but in our understanding of the meaning of the underlying processes involved. In other words, this becomes a philosophical question as to how we attribute certain values to any given process or, more specifically, how something comes to be viewed as pathological within any given society. I should like to end this chapter by highlighting some of these ideas from an anthropological perspective.

Frazer (1957) defined magic as based on two principles of thought: first, that like produces like, leading to the law of similarity or homeopathic magic; second, that things which have once been in contact continue to act upon each other even when no contact is apparent, leading to the law of contagion. Frazer considered that these laws governing the association of ideas originated in external causality. This provides an interesting example of how certain ideas may be culturally significant (e.g. God created the world in six days) but, in a totally different context, a different set of assumptions is called upon. The issue of external causality for the disturbed person has been interpreted by psychoanalytic theory as the necessity of taking back into the self what is seen in this context as projected parts of the self which have been located externally, thereby weakening the strength of the ego.

Whereas I am highlighting the potential for confusion and fear in the non-differentiation of self and object or thought and action, Frazer gives an example of the curative potential of magical ideas:

> One of the great merits of homeopathic magic is that it enables the cure to be performed on the person of the doctor instead of his victim who is thus relieved of all trouble and inconvenience, while he sees his medical man writhe in anguish before him. For example, the peasants of Pershe, in France, labour under the impression that a prolonged fit of vomiting is brought about by the patient's stomach becoming unhooked . . . and so falling down. Accordingly a practitioner is called to restore the organ to its proper place. After hearing the symptoms, he at once throws himself into the most horrible contortions for the purpose of unhooking his own stomach. Having succeeded in the effort he next hooks it up again in another series of contortions and grimaces, while the patient experiences a corresponding relief. Fee 5 francs.
>
> (Frazer 1957)

He gives other examples of cultures in which, for instance, a pregnant woman may not spin or twist ropes for two months before her delivery, lest the child's guts become entangled like the thread. With relation to food, he relates a belief in the connection between the food in a person's stomach and that which is left uneaten: by interfering with the latter, one could injure the eater. These notions that influencing things which are external to the body has an effect on, or inside, the body itself may be linked to many of the concepts regarding magical ideas and more specifically to those ideas about the body.

Piaget criticized Frazer for not differentiating between the animistic ideas of primitive peoples and those of children, while social anthropologist Mary Douglas condemned his disregard of the distinction between primitive and modern culture: 'If he had not been convinced that savages think on entirely different lines from ourselves, he might have been content to treat magic as symbolic action' (Douglas 1966). Nevertheless, despite these criticisms and the fact that many of Frazer's ideas are today considered very outmoded, I believe that the underlying principles of magic thinking that he expounds are very enlightening.

Douglas's discussion of magical ideas in their cultural context has helped me to make sense of this area. Unlike Frazer, she does not differentiate on the basis of science versus symbolism. Instead, she suggests that we do not carry forward the same set of symbols from one context to the next. She constantly questions whether primitive cultures resort to bodily magic to achieve their desires and whether such cultural rites are interpreted as if they express the same preoccupations that fill the minds of psychopaths or infants. This is precisely what I am suggesting that patients in western cultures, who are suffering from eating disorders, attempt to do. In opposition to this, Brown (1959) states that in primitive culture there is a low degree of sublimation, producing a weaker ego, which in turn leads to the fantastic wishes of infantile narcissism. These wishes are expressed in unsublimated form, so that 'man retains the magic body of infancy', which is associated with the confusion between the internal and external world.

The argument, therefore, is whether these connections between people and events, which characterize primitive culture, do derive from similar developmental failures as those which I shall be examining further with regards to the patients in this book. Is their magic also based on failure to differentiate?

By now the reader may have begun to consider some of the ways in which magical ideas can serve both the individual and society and to appreciate the contribution made by both psychology and anthropology to informing our understanding. Later, we are going to be focusing on magic concerning ideas about the body. Douglas describes the way in which rituals and certain behaviours enacted on the body may be used to 'confront or master' painful experience. Whilst there are various ways of understanding this, we must be aware of her emphasis on the dangers of shifting our interpretation of social concerns on to personal ones. Similarly, Evans-Pritchard (1976) warned of the deformation of thought that is risked by the

interpreter who is determined to make everything somehow transla-
table.

His comment referred to the interpretation of magic in terms of
the weakness inherent in primitive mental functioning. However, I
include it to highlight another area of concern. In this book I am
talking about different uses of language: that of the concrete and the
symbolic, the personal and the societal, the conscious and the
unconscious and, with regard to art therapy, the verbal and the
visual. It is impossible to expect to be able always to find adequate
equations or translations between these systems. A basic respect for
the language system used by any individual or group necessitates an
acceptance that there can never be only one version of meaning.
This will be developed further in the next chapter.

Chapter 2

Magic and eating

Food has always played a crucial role in the activities of all cultures, both ancient and modern. Famine and gluttony, voluntary abstinence from food, the interrelationship between food and the body, and the handling of food involve well-recorded rituals and all have significance for the understanding of women patients with eating disorders.

Bruch (1974) comments upon tribes in which both famines and the practice of gluttony are commonplace. A Trobriand islander, anticipating a feast in the south-west Pacific says: 'We shall be glad; we shall eat until we vomit'. A South African tribal expression is: 'We shall eat, until our bellies swell out and we can no longer stand.' This anticipation of feasting and over-eating seems to suggest an underlying threat of starvation. It is as if one is always connected to the other. One is reminded of Pharaoh's dream of seven fat cows eaten by seven thin cows and Joseph's interpretation of this as seven years of plenty to be followed by seven years of famine and drought. As Joseph prepares for the famine during the years of plenty he is rewarded by Pharaoh. This kind of thoughtfulness and forward planning is not at all the same as the sheer indulgence and excessive over-eating of the Romans. The building of vomitoriums allowed them to relieve themselves by vomiting as a socially acceptable custom. However, one assumes that the consumption of vast quantities of food was not associated with the feelings of disgust, panic and depression, sometimes leading to suicidal thoughts, of those suffering from bulimia. Amongst women with eating disorders in western societies, the real or imagined threat of emotional starvation or famine may produce a response similar to that of gluttony. However, it is important to stress that it is not necessarily the behaviour or action itself which implies a certain meaning but the context in which that behaviour occurs.

Voluntary abstinence from food is a common religious tradition. It is a means to liberate the self from selfish and materialistic concerns, a concrete purification of body and soul. Both Yom Kippur, the Jewish Day of Atonement, and the Christian period of Lent invite fasting or restriction for the purpose of atonement or penitence.

Abstaining from food may also achieve empowerment. In ancient Japan a man could humiliate his enemy by 'fasting against him', or starving on his doorstep. In India Gandhi refused to take food during his struggle for the independence of India. He is reported to have said of his act: 'there cannot be any pure decision to starve oneself to death [because of] a paradoxical combination of passionate belief in the absolute vitality of certain living issues . . . and the determination to die for them' (Bruch 1974). There is a similar paradox in the anorectic's refusal to eat: for her, it represents a means of survival.

Specific foods also carry 'magical' significance. Transubstantiation has a long history and is often observed within a religious context. The magical conversion of bread into flesh was customary amongst the Aryans of Ancient India. Their priests could turn bread into the very body of their god. By eating it, they were taking into themselves a part of his divine substance. Similarly, the early Brahmans taught that rice cakes, which were offered in sacrifice as substitutes for humans, were actually converted into human bodies by the priest: the rice cake alone was the hair; when water was added, the skin was thus created; and when rice cake and water were mixed together, the flesh was created. Transubstantiation was also practised by the Aztecs. Today the custom of eating bread sacramentally is part of the Catholic doctrine in which the one body of Christ is present during all masses carried out simultaneously.

Magical ideas may concern the preservation of food supplies. Douglas describes how amongst the Nyakyusa in Africa it is thought that a pregnant woman who comes near a supply of grain reduces the quantity of grain as she approaches because the foetus inside her is so voracious and is able to snatch it. The people describe the foetus as having 'jaws agape' and they talk of the seed within fighting the seed without: 'The child in the belly . . . is like a witch, and will damage food like witchcraft' (Douglas 1966).

Many fascinating examples of magical ideas which are related to eating processes exist in a variety of cultures and religions. For instance, in certain parts of India and in Polynesia, mere contact with food or the process of cooking food is considered to be the start of ingestion. This gives rise to certain strict taboos. Douglas tells of the Havik tribe of Mysore for whom the actual process of eating is regarded as potentially defiling. For this tribe, all saliva, even one's own, is impure. Since sitting side by side at a meal spreads contamination, everyone is seated separately.

Predominent in the thinking of patients with eating disorders is the need to be separate, to create extra boundaries between themselves and objects which may lead to danger through contact. Similarly, for an anorectic, the significance of accepting food from a parent touches on ideas concerning the actual incorporation of another person. The foundations for these ideas differ dramatically, however.

Understanding the nature of the boundary between inside the body and outside the body is essential in order not only to make sense of the dilemmas facing patients with eating disorders but also to shed more light on their need to use magical thinking.

The symbolism of the body or body contents may be seen to have a magic of its own. In many societies certain clothes or ornaments, such as a military uniform or a judge's wig, are assumed magically to bestow extra power upon the wearer. Campbell (1929) suggests that some societies attribute significance directly to these objects but that others require that the wearer's body itself must be changed. Worldwide, there are examples of mutilations of the body (e.g. circumcision, piercing), each of which carries symbolic meaning for the group within which it is practised. For the anorectic, the visual effect of the transformation in her body conveys symbolic meaning too, because a certain body shape is associated culturally with a particular meaning. Schilder (1970) notes that primitive magic is often connected with specific parts of the body and especially with those which have a libidinal significance.

Marion, the central character in Margaret Atwood's book *The Edible Woman*, is an ordinary woman who, having just left University, is hoping to get married. She finds herself literally unable to 'stomach' the life that she expects for herself, where women become the very things that they take in to themselves. Pondering on the women who were celebrating Christmas with her, Marion concluded:

What Peculiar Creatures they were. The continual flux between the outside and the inside, taking things in, giving them out, chewing, words, potato chips, burps, grease, hair, babies, milk, excrement, cookies, vomit, coffee, tomato juice, blood, tea, sweat, liquor, tears and garbage.

(Atwood 1980)

Her musings tended towards the animistic:

She became aware of the carrot. It's a root, she thought. It grows in the ground and sends up leaves. Then they come along and dig it up, maybe it even makes a sound, a scream too low for us to hear, but it doesn't die right away, it keeps on living, right now it's still alive.

(Atwood 1980)

These passages introduce the idea of the taboo against (or at least the discomfort arising from) eating something which is in some way akin to oneself. Such ideas, verging on the animistic or the magical, are common amongst patients with eating disorders and set them apart from everyone else. Deviations from any cultural norm, which serve no social function but only the needs of the individual, show how magical ideas can become pathological.

Bruch (1974) describes a schizophrenic girl who over-ate. The girl described frightening feelings to do with other people's anger. Their words would rattle around inside her and keep wounding her. By eating she believed that she would cover her sore inside like a poultice and thereby would literally feel no hurt.

Restricting the intake of food has psychological as well as physiological effects, amongst which is a temporary euphoria. This 'feeds in' to the belief of the anorectic that her body has special magical qualities, for example that she can walk forever. Her only weakness is her mind, which she can split from her body and which allows her to assume the armour of immortality.

Owing to this sense of having a separate body, the anorectic often describes feeling full when she has eaten nothing at all but has served food to others and watched them eat. These convoluted thoughts, based on the process of identification, may also allow her to feel that other people can do the eating for her.

Food as a solid object is fantasized about in a variety of ways. Anorectics frequently express the idea that the food remains solid after eating, and therefore becomes a part of them (see Figure 2.1).

Figure 2.1

From there it is not a great leap for these patients to make the association between eating food and eating people. The food itself takes on the power that a person might have, as if the food were animated and could in some way force the patient to eat it.

This fantasy has so often been expressed in art therapy sessions, either directly in relation to the painted images or indirectly through fantasies of swallowing the materials themselves, that I began to question the nature of the relationship between these animistic ideas about food, the fantasies about eating a person, and such severe disturbances in eating, and to ponder how this could be worked with through the use of art therapy (see Figures 2.2 and 2.3).

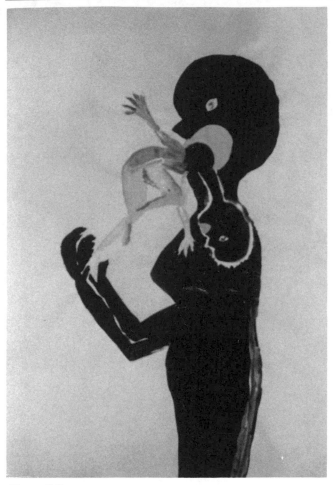

Figure 2.2

It is not only eating but also purging and vomiting that are attributed with magical qualities. Rosen and Leitenberg (1985) contrast bulimics with the classic obsessive-compulsive hand washers, as regards contact with a potentially contaminating substance (i.e. food). They describe how the latter group tries to avoid initial contact with contaminated substances, perhaps because hand washing never completely resolves the dread of contamination. Bulima nervosa patients on the other hand, seem somehow to be more secure in the magical protection of vomiting.

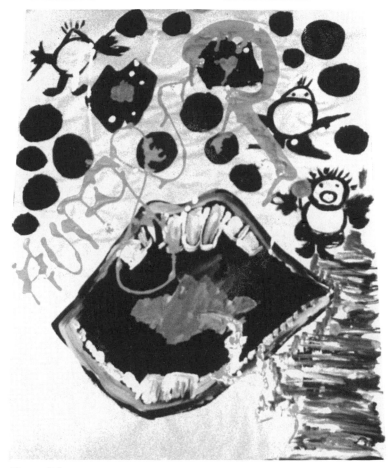

Figure 2.3

In this way too, patients with eating disorders attempt to feel that they have ultimate control over what goes into their bodies and what comes out. The issue becomes more complex when one appreciates the paradoxical nature of food, which may be experienced simultaneously as comforting yet intrusive and invasive. When food is felt to be persecutory, it cannot be allowed to contaminate the body or to become part of it. In this state of mind, the patient needs to control everything which may impinge on the outside or inside of the body. A further complication is what is meant by the word 'everything'. Owing to the tendency to use concrete rather than symbolic thoughts, the vulnerable patient may experience words or the therapist's interpretations as, say, a punch in the stomach, as something which can impinge on her bodily self and against which she must therefore defend herself.

Chapter 3

Magical control of the body

A child or an adult tries to influence external events by magic only when he/she has no other way of acting on them. Similarly, a patient with an eating disorder feels quite unable to affect things around her by any other means. Frequently she feels that she has no 'voice' within her family and that she has little sense of self. Her potential for self-direction or for having an effect on others is diminished by her sense of being practically invisible. Her only power is a magical one, to control what no others can – her own body.

It was through being made to feel helpless in relation to some of these patients that I began to question how their magical control arose. I was told over and over again that no one could possibly help them, that no one could understand their artwork or help them to think differently about their bodies.

The means of 'magical control' may vary: the frantic need to cleanse the body of its contents before they might produce untold damage or the compulsive urge to reduce the size of the body in order to find a separate identity. Both of these, however, encapsulate the idea of gaining control over a body which is experienced as helpless in relation to others and to its own functions. The individual is living out a desire to control both the internal and external world; to protect herself from abandonment or annihilation by means of her own omnipotence.

Our first efforts, both magical and realistic, to master the world and to make it serve our needs are focused on our mother's body. Within the fantasy of controlling the self, therefore, may also be included that of controlling the mother. The compulsive dieter, who is aware in some way of her early experiences of helplessness (waiting to be fed, needs as yet unmet), can now be in full control of those areas of her life by granting or withholding her body's needs and can also exert a powerful influence over others.

Chernin (1983) suggests that, whereas men may rape or abuse women partially as an expression of their rage at having been powerless in relation to their mothers, women may express this rage within their own bodies. To quote the heroine of *Lady Oracle* by Margaret Atwood: 'The war between myself and my mother was on in earnest; the disputed territory was my body' (Atwood 1982).

The point at issue is: who *owns* the anorectic's body, and so who has the power to put things in it, either by feeding or by influence? For many patients, the potential catastrophe involved in submitting to the will of another necessitates a controlling of all interactions. At stake is the autonomy, the existence, of the person as an individual. How is the issue of autonomy and separateness related to magical ideas about eating?

From birth, the infant is helpless, in the power of another on whom he/she depends for satisfaction of hunger, for warmth, and for all other bodily needs. The wish to be in total control of these areas may therefore be seen as an attempt to avoid not only the need for or dependency on another but also the risk of such needs not being met.

Guntrip (1982) defines anorexia as 'hardly so much a symptom as a guiding principle of life'. He quotes the dream of a patient which consisted of endless meals. When food was available, however, this patient lost interest in it, just as she lost interest in her husband on his return home, despite having longed for him all day. Guntrip explains these experiences as the patient's way of denying her great neediness.

The defiant assertion by the anorectic that she needs nothing from anyone conceals great ambivalence. This defiance conveys the outward expression of 'no needs', combined with obvious signals of great need. The enormous hunger for care and for relationships is denied, through fear of being abused, deceived or made utterly dependent. Within the context of a precarious sense of self, which requires tremendous effort to establish a sense of identity, such a hunger may often be satisfied by striving to obtain her own special, unique, thinness.

Kleinian psychoanalysts highlight the importance of envy in such cases. These patients envy those who appear to them to have the capacity to fulfil the need for care and relationships. Envy contributes to the infant's difficulties in building up good objects, as he/

she feels that the good things of which he/she was deprived were deliberately kept from him/her. Envy also deeply affects the capacity for gratitude and happiness. One of the unconscious aims of envy is to destroy another's creativeness. The adult patient, knowing that she devalues the help being offered, may then feel unworthy of it and full of guilt.

For these patients, the body itself is involved in the expression of conflict, partly because of the mechanism of displacement and the limited capacity to symbolize. This limited capacity results in bodily metaphors being used rather than psychological ones. The individual is therefore thrown back on to the first line of defence, namely the use of her own body. Emotional conflict may, in concrete fashion, be experienced physically: the conflict, for which the patient may not even have words, is demonstrated more 'primitively' through action. The patient with an eating disorder therefore uses her body in a perverse way.

Although the refusal to eat by the anorectic may be understood in terms of the *symbolic* attachment to her mother, this may be experienced at a more primitive level. The anorectic may experience a direct attachment to her mother's body as the two bodies are not fully differentiated. The attachment may also be related to the tremendous desire to possess the mother again, recalling the way in which her food was once able to produce satisfaction and contentment, and to be at one with her. Now this must be achieved by the patient's own omnipotence.

However, the desire to re-merge, to fuse with the mother or with the therapist (in a therapeutic relationship) carries with it the fear of being engulfed, swallowed up, annihilated. If the individual tries to protect herself by creating a greater distance/space between herself and the feared object, she has to face the fear of abandonment and isolation. The patient with an eating disorder seems to lack flexibility within her relationships, since both extremes of relating to another are dangerously close. This concept has been described by M. Glasser, psychoanalyst at the Portman Clinic, London as the 'core complex' in perverse personalities. Such opposing forces result in the anorectic's desperate need to control her environment and relationships. Having observed this myself, I was led to question how these patients deal with this and in what way, if any, this conflict is related to attempts at magical control.

Magical control is necessary in relation to not only the external figures in the patient's life but also her internal representations of these figures. Like the drug addict who says 'I can take this, I can control it, it won't control me', the patient's belief in her magical degree of omnipotence over the symbolic material object is profound. Her desire is to be able to satisfy the need on demand and to believe too that the object of satisfaction can be given up at will. Symbolically this may be understood as the ability both to take in the mother and to push her out at will. However, it should not be understood in terms of either some magical means of recapturing a state of infancy or a fear of adulthood. On the contrary, according to Selvini Palazzoli, desire for autonomy is the key factor, regardless of the direction of growth: 'Emaciation [becomes] the magic key to greater power' (1974). The infant's experience of his/her mother is simultaneously nutritional and emotional; the physical and mental feelings are inextricably linked. For the patient with an eating disorder, incorporating her mother emotionally must occur concretely, on the physical level. Thus, the means to expel her from the body includes vomiting her out.

By means of the omnipotence of thoughts, magic seeks to gratify those very aspects of narcissism which reality forces us to realize are not capable of being satisfied. Magical control is the only means by which these patients feel that they can survive having and being a body.

Sours (1980) describes the anorectic's perception as:

a passive helpless object which is easily invaded or taken over by outside forces. Intrusions from the unknown. She sees food and her mother as potential instruments of control. She believes that she lacks the will power, perceiving herself as passable – receptive, anxious and powerless. Her body is not authentic. It is not hers. *It is vulnerable to invasion and parental misuses. She can return to a feeling of immense power only by separating flesh from her body through an act of will* . . . otherwise fear will seep into her like stain, parts of her will drift in and out, nothing will remain but the same old question: 'Does she exist?'

(Sours 1980; emphasis added)

The words in italics highlight two important points which will be discussed later: first, the potential for feeling invaded, which will be linked to the concept of psychic cannibalism; second, the mind and body split which is very much part of the self-perception of the patient with an eating disorder (see Figure 3.1).

In anorectics may be found a desire for a numinous reality, free of

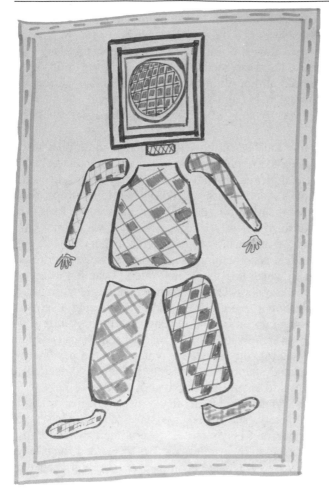

Figure 3.1

the limitations of ordinary experience, which in some ways is comparable to our ideas about shamans or prophets. The existence of a mystic is dominated by discipline and restraint and often comprises a severe regime of mortification of the flesh, including fasting and chastity. This deprivation of basic needs is, however, apparently compensated for by the joy of mystical experience.

Selvini Palazzoli quotes a Catholic theologian on the spiritual experience of fasting:

the spirit becomes more sensitive, more far seeing and more acute and the conscience more quick and lively . . . the awareness of spiritual power is increased and with it the danger of losing sight of what is assigned to each one of us, the limits of our finite existence, of our dignity and our abilities. Hence the dangers of pride, magic and spiritual intoxication.

(Selvini Palazzoli 1974)

This description touches on an issue which is more relevant to existentialism than to psychoanalytic psychotherapy, namely the desire for spiritual development. In the 'twelve-step' literature used by Alcoholics Anonymous and other such fellowships, there is a recognition of the need for spiritual principles in our lives. The starting point for this is merely a recognition that we are not God. Whether or not we have or we develop a belief in God, the acceptance that there is something greater than ourselves addresses the very danger to which this theologian refers. Learning to accept our limits, our powerlessness and our human qualities is intrinsically linked both to becoming more human and to developing a spiritual awareness. The more an individual expends energy on splitting off parts of his/her awareness of aspects of the self, because these aspects are too painful, the less there remains of the personality. With such a depleted state of the self, the patient is compelled to resort to any means to ensure the survival of the rest of herself.

The patient with an eating disorder makes use of magical thinking to feel safe. Ultimately, she becomes a slave to both her way of thinking and her aberrant behaviour. The very internal freedom for which she is so desperately searching on her misguided route fades further and further away as she becomes ever more entrenched in her cycle of addiction. Similarly, the alcoholic or drug addict yearns to be at peace with him/herself, to be able to exist alone and also in relation to others. He/she searches for these elusive means of living his/her life at the bottom of a bottle of whisky or inside a syringe, and so the real world is progressively shunned, as is the potential acceptance of his/her humanity.

An anorectic patient said of her painting of an angel that it represented her ideal self. She described it as an incorporeal heavenly being and poignantly conveyed her intense wish to deny her bodily self. Many shamanistic practices involve attempts at overcoming the human condition.

Buddhist monks are instructed to meditate upon the nine apertures from which 'filthy and repulsive substances flow increasingly'. Psychological theories relate the disgust with the body to the fascination of the infant with his/her own bodily products, such as excrement, and the strict repression of this. However, the forbidden images remain and may reassert their force. Hence, filth becomes associated with sin and purity with virtue. A heaven and hell exists in some form within all religions.

The mind–body split is not confined to the realm of psychopathology. There is an important social dimension. Chernin (1983) describes how in the Renaissance women were considered less capable of controlling their lust, gluttony, anger and greed than were men. As far back as the first six centuries of the Christian era, writers dwelt upon the 'vexation of marriage' and reviled the body.

Another split which exists between the mind and body is also culture-bound. Frazer (1957) describes primitive man taking his soul out of his body and depositing it for security in some snug spot, just as people deposit their money with a banker rather than carry it on their person. Should he discover a place of absolute security, he may be content to leave his soul there permanently and so ensure his immortality.

These different ways of thinking about the relationship between mind and body help us to understand more about the nature of the eating-disordered patient's experience of herself. Psychoanalytic theory suggests that the development of the personality is based largely on the individual's relationship with her own body, from the time that she perceives it as a whole entity, existing outside the maternal object. Freud says that the ego is first and foremost a bodily ego. The acceptance of the body is crucial to healthy development. In patients with an eating disorder, however, we see an accentuation of a schism between the mind and body in an attempt to deny the body's very existence.

Selvini Palazzoli (1974) suggests that the anorectic, rather than being afraid of food, is afraid of her own body and experiences the intake of food as an increase of her body at the expense of her ego. Food is therefore a body substance. 'Being a body is tantamount to being a thing. As it grows, the person shrinks! '

What is it about the increase of body mass that, for the anorectic, is equated with loss of self? This can be partially explained by recalling the patient's problem with symbolization and separation. The anorectic does not feel merely that her growing body contains the bad object, rather she feels that *she is* the bad object. Very often self-portraits painted by such patients serve to make them aware of their confusion over whether they have depicted their own body or that of their mother.

The body is therefore experienced concretely as the maternal object, from which the ego wishes to separate itself at all costs. The patient feels enslaved by her own body and fights back by resisting its signals, thereby attempting to differentiate herself from her own body.

This poses an interesting question regarding the relationship of these patients with their own bodies. Is the anorectic strongly 'embodied', that is, inextricably bound up with her body, its sensations and its limitations, or is she unembodied, that is, detached from her body in the way in which R. D. Laing (1960) describes in his book *The Divided Self*? Palazzoli suggests that these patients are highly embodied from the start and that this is partially the cause of their unhappiness. Schizophrenics on the other hand have a body schema which is disturbed precisely because they do not experience their body as their own.

The psychotic person has an ever-changing experience of parts of his/her body. Without awareness, he/she exists out of the body, in fragments. The patient with an eating disorder at least has the notion of her body as a container and the less disturbed eating-disordered patient has some consistent experience of a body. However, the extent to which she may rely upon psychotic mechanisms, such as the use of splitting, will affect the extent to which she is able to have any sense of continuity of herself, whether of her psychological self or her bodily self.

The eating-disordered patient with a severe disturbance has a perception of her own and of others' bodies which can be seen to exist in parts or fragments. Her attempts to escape the physical constraints of being bound to her body are often expressed in violent attacks upon the body, either literally or in art form (see Figure 3.2). Examples of this may be seen in such patients' artwork and throughout the therapeutic relationship, as patients with an eating disorder frequently describe that they do not feel as if they exist inside their bodies. This may be portrayed in self-images which emphasize the head and neglect or attack the body.

This leads to the question of whether it is the potential experience of the total body and soul as an integrated whole that must be defended against, and therefore splitting occurs in order to avoid

Figure 3.2

experiencing a variety of different feelings. It is possible that the primary anxiety is based in the fragments of the self and that any actual increase in body weight means that the anorectic has to tolerate even more of her experience of the intolerable body and self. If this is the case, she will be working hard to deny her enslaved state of embodiment.

The body is experienced as an object quite separate from the spirit. It is something to be owned or used and is not felt to be the very essence of the self. The patient expresses the Cartesian dichotomy: she believes the mind transcends her body and so offers her unlimited power over her own behaviour and that of others.

There appears to be a very important link between the way in which these patients use, or more precisely abuse, their bodies and their own (perhaps not yet recognized) experience of having been used or abused by others. In the same way as self-mutilators often describe being able to attack their own bodies viciously, as if they were hunks of flesh with no human connection, patients with eating disorders may disassociate their true selves from their bodies. The eating-disordered patient can then treat her body as a separate object as cruelly as she wishes. In this way she can temporarily believe that she is in full control of this body object.

Another very important way in which these patients attempt to exert control is in relation to space. Frequently, the bulimic patient experiences intense anxiety about space. (This will be discussed in more detail in the chapters on the use of art therapy.) She is concerned about the empty space inside herself and frantically tries to fill it up. The 'spaces' left when no activity is taking place may intensify her experience of 'being nothing' or 'not existing'. The 'spaces' left in the silences between people's conversations may be intolerable. She is constantly on the run from experiencing 'gaps' and 'spaces'. The more borderline the functioning, the more concretely this anxiety may be expressed. For example, through the body, many patients experience physically that their skin is not providing a secure enough container, that their bodily pores are open too wide and that, both inside and outside, empty spaces leave gaping holes which have to be filled.

These experiences may lead to a variety of addictive behaviours, such as binge eating. Many bulimic patients are also aware that they may use other substances, such as alcohol or drugs, or indulge in behaviour such as self-mutilation, sex or even overwork to fill the gaps. Needing other people to fill up the spaces may feel like the only way in which the patient is able to define herself, in relation to others, when her very existence is in doubt. It is a form of co-dependency. Thus, the need to exert control over both internal and external space affords some measure of control over her identity. What she is really attempting to achieve through these various desperate means is a sense of continuity of herself and a feeling of connectedness to significant others. Because of the nature of the splitting process she is unable naturally to maintain her self-image, or the image of another person, in an ongoing, sustaining way.

Chapter 4

Body boundaries in patients with eating disorders

Establishing boundaries is a dynamic process, involving the way in which the other person, originally the mother, is experienced as different and therefore as separate from the self. The earliest experience of the infant has been described as a state of symbiotic fusion. Separation is intricately linked to the development of the boundaries of the self. In early infancy it functions to distinguish the self from the not-self. The development of boundaries means demarcation and structure and therefore containment of the self. This in turn leads to a relationship with what is the not-self, to an awareness of inner and outer processes and spaces and also, significantly, of time. What is interesting about the art process is that creative activity depends upon the ability to distinguish between subject and object and yet at the same time allow enough flexibility of ego boundaries to relate both what is known and what is not known.

An important factor in considering boundary development concerns the experience of the body. Winnicott (1980) locates the psyche in the whole body whereas Schilder (1970) goes even further. He believes that whatever originates in or emanates from our body remains a part of the body image, even when it is separated in space from the body. This might include the voice, the breath, odour or faeces.

The body-ego, as a precursor to every other aspect of development, is originally based upon identification with the mother's body and the first awareness of limitations. Physical contact with the mother presents the infant with basic realities, such as an awareness of his/her own capacity to take in or to reject the mother's milk. This relationship forms the rudiments of the infant's understanding of what occurs between two bodies. Since, at the start, the infant's recognition of inside and outside and therefore of self and other is not fully established, it is understandable that the infant cannot accurately locate the provider of his/her bodily satisfactions. This lack of differentiation may prove a devastating experience for the infant when the mother is absent, because he/she is initially not able to distinguish the absence of the other from that of a part of his/her own body. In later life this experience may be expressed in a variety of ways, but especially, through bodily sensations of 'holes' or 'something missing inside' which, it is felt, must be responded to by having the same, physical, presence of something. That something, which is used to 'fill the gap', may be an excessive dependency on relationships or on substances, including food.

It is important to distinguish between the development of a boundary and that of a barrier. The patient with an eating disorder, whilst frantically attempting to fill the gaps that she feels exist within her own body (either through bingeing or anorectically resisting that same need), is actually creating a barrier, a self-container. For her, the failure to establish a secure body-ego leads to severe difficulties in developing a concept as insubstantial as a boundary, which may both link her to and separate her from her object.

The patient veers between protecting herself from experiencing a devastating emptiness, when she ensures that nothing or no one can penetrate her brittle barrier, and fearing that she will be totally wiped out if she lets things or people into her (see Figure 4.1). While the processes involved in eating may well be experienced as food managing to cross the body barrier, an alternative threat lies in not eating, in experiencing hunger. To experience hunger, just as an addict suffers a craving, forces the patient to recognize that there is something (which may not yet be distinguished from food or drugs) outside of herself which she desperately wants. This implies that she is a separate object from the wanted thing or person and the experience of not having it or the person under her control, meeting her needs on demand, may be quite intolerable.

The way in which the body-ego is formed will influence the nature of all relationships. If the process of realizing one's separate existence is experienced as being literally cut off from the body to which one is connected, then being separate may feel like being in space or being confronted with nothingness or even death. It may be from one of these places that the patient with an eating disorder has to run in order to find something that will reconnect her. The process

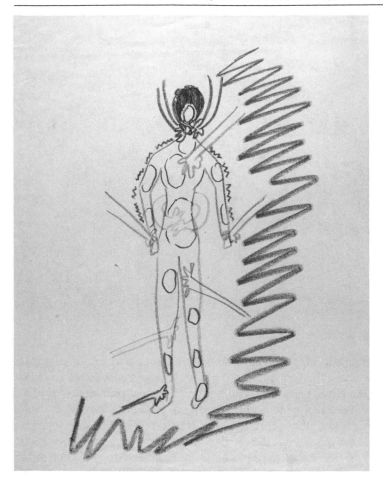

Figure 4.1

of putting food or chemicals into her body may recreate an early experience of being connected to the mother and therefore kept alive.

Although the individual may be driven by her need to possess and incorporate the other, her terror of being in touch with her own devouring needs restricts her. Even if she successfully manages (as many of these patients do) to sustain an image of independence and self-sufficiency, inwardly she is constantly battling to control the devourer (see Figure 4.2).

The identity of the devourer will be considered later in relation to

Figure 4.2

cannibalistic ideas. Meanwhile, it is important to try to understand more about the formation of the body image. From infancy we take into ourselves parts of others' body images and push out parts of our own. The development of the body image occurs in parallel to that of perception, thoughts and object relations. The less developed the body image, the greater is the tendency toward transformations: parts of the body appear not to be connected with each other, making it easier to expel them and to take in other parts. This particular way of understanding body image and body boundary refers not to separate, static or objectively measurable phenomena but to personalized ideas about the body and its boundaries.

The body image is not necessarily confined by the actual boundaries of the physical body but often expands beyond it, into space. Indeed, during early development there is a continual testing out to discover what might be incorporated into the body. The so-called 'distorted body perceptions' of patients with eating disorders are often measurements of actual or perceived body outline. These perceptions do not lead to an understanding of the fragmented nature of the body image and the lack of a coherent sense of bodily self which changes in shape and content. These fluctuations and inconsistencies with regard to the body are predominant features of eating disorders and are linked to certain magical ideas of incorporating another person into a body which already feels so variable. The image of the body is built up then dissolved and built up again. In different states of mind, such as dreaming, the body may become changeable, plastic or even transportable.

From an anthropological perspective on the social aspects of the body, Douglas (1973) describes the desire to incorporate oneself into a patterned social world, to push back the boundary between inside and outside, which may be achieved through a variety of rituals. She suggests that controls are exerted by the social system, which places limits on the use of the body as a medium for expression. We should always expect some concordance between social and bodily expressions of, say, control, because each symbolic mode enhances meaning in the other. This accounts for her idea that interest in the body apertures depends upon the preoccupation with social exits and entrances, escape routes and invasions. She goes on to suggest that we should not expect to find concern with bodily boundaries if there were no concern to preserve social boundaries. She thereby creates a coherent link between the individual (or part of) and the wider social network.

These ideas are extremely interesting in relation to the history of sexual abuse. Today an adult or a child has the right to expect that his/her body will not be invaded or controlled by another. This was not always the case. Depending upon the social context in which people related to each other, for instance when slavery was widespread, personal ownership of one's body could not be taken for granted. History shows us that we have the capacity to function in systems in which one human being owns another.

How we make sense psychologically, socially, historically or otherwise of these systems begs the question of our capacity to respect any individual in the way that we would wish to be respected ourselves. People who have been used as objects in some way themselves, with their own physical and emotional needs unrecognized, may unconsciously make use of others as what has been termed narcissistic self-objects. Their children, for instance, may be used to fulfil their own needs. A needy mother unintentionally inhibits the child's recognition of what is 'not me', and therefore his/her subsequent gradual acceptance of dependency, by not facilitating the child's need for growing independence. Instead, she mirrors the child's dependency on her, which is what *she* needs, rather than providing a maternal object from which the child can become independent in order to fulfil the child's needs.

In order to be able to respond empathically to the needs or wishes of another, we have to be able to allow the other to initiate object relations. If the mother or indeed the therapist is motivated by her own need for control to make use of the child or the patient, no basic acknowledgement of or respect for the other is present. The way in which all activities and interactions are carried out between people conveys something of this. A child being stuffed with food will be more likely to experience a sensation of being invaded, of help-lessness, than one of having the needs of hunger met. Similarly therapists can be experienced in the same way through their use of interpretations, the food that they offer to their patients.

Douglas (1973) describes how the demands for strong bodily control are greater when social control is strong. She comments on how elements of this are played out within the families of anorectics, where the physical body is in conflict with the social body. Recognition of the aesthetic benefits for the body, the more it is controlled, is certainly not the monopoly of the anorectic. Many of Plato's ideas, described by Thevoz (1984), develop this theme. Plato believes that the body can attain true beauty only through self-discipline, that man is called upon to ajdust himself physically to the idealized image of himself provided by the artist. This is an interesting concept in that it suggests that a wished-for image of the self may be influenced by external images. Schilder (1970), however, takes a psychoanalytic view in the idea that the body image develops as the infant tries to integrate internal and external stimuli, which may become identical with the earliest objects. In other words, part of the body self is built up in response to the needs of the personality. It appears that the physical sensations experi-enced within the body have no inner meaning until they are connected up with the body image. This is of particular relevance to patients with eating disorders, who demonstrate a lack of ability in recognizing signals from their own bodies, such as awareness of hunger.

Rose (1964) describes the body image as being symbolized in a magical archaic way, so that all objects, relationships and feelings come to be experienced in actual physical changes, resulting in an image of one's body. Thus, at this very early stage of body image symbolism, actual bodily feelings and sensations come to signify the gratifications and frustrations that were experienced in relationship to the mother.

Without a firmly established and secure edge to the body, growth can be frightening. As the body becomes bigger and bigger, in an uncontrolled way, the anorectic patient tries variously to create boundaries for herself. The badness inside (concretely thought of as the food itself rather than internalized bad objects) appears to grow at the same rate as the developing body. Sometimes, therefore, she has to resort to using very rigid defences internally because the external body feels as if it were open to invasion or being devoured by an internal agency.

Many of these patients have difficulty in distinguishing between what is contained inside themselves and what is outside. This leads to much anxiety regarding taking anything in. Bingeing is one way of attempting to create a self-boundary. Patients often describe having eaten so much that they reach their limit. Their experience of reaching limits or boundaries is so elusive that only the physical stretching of the stomach wall provides them with some concrete semblance of boundary.

The lack of a boundaried body is described in an example given by Bruch (1974). A 14-year-old obese boy was terrified of sustaining any injuries because he did not believe what he had learned in biology lessons about the human body. He felt that his body was full of jelly or pea soup and that, if he were injured, it would all 'come tumbling out', leaving a balloon of skin around his bones. He would be totally empty. The very thought caused him to eat frantically.

Poor boundaries may, in certain instances, lead to the need to protect that which is inside, to defend vigorously against outside intrusion. One anorectic patient painted a small country cottage. The image was fairly typical of paintings produced by anorectics in the early stages of treatment, in that it was very neat, idealistic and romanticized. This house had pretty curtains, drawn across each window, and a large lock on the front door. The front gate was firmly closed. The patient described how she felt that she was inside this house and no one could get in.

It appeared that the house symbolized her body and that the issue of entry was concerned with crossing boundaries. Her perception of entry into this house was that it would have to be forced since there was no easy access. It did not occur to her that she might allow someone inside. Rather, she felt that she was under threat of being invaded. At the same time she appeared to be communicating a message to me, which I understood to be: 'I won't let you inside me.' I encouraged her to develop a fantasy around this house, in which she said that she would leave it only to empty the rubbish. I understood this to mean: 'I choose when and what I throw out [up]!' She was talking about having control over what entered her body and what left it, a tenuous dividing line for her which necessitated fierce protection.

The patient with an eating disorder creates images in her mind of fortresses, such as fences, walls and/or fierce dogs. Also, psychological fortresses, in the guise of phobias or obsessions, are created as defences to protect the vulnerable boundary to the body. For much of the time what she feels that she is protecting herself against is food. Since she regards her thoughts as magical in effect, her wish is to satisfy herself without any consequences upon her body. The reality with which she is faced is that food does affect her body, and so food becomes invested with power.

Food becomes almost like a demand which has to be curtailed and controlled at all costs. One anorectic refused to stand near a fridge because of an obsessional idea that calories might somehow escape from inside it and work their way into her. This near-psychotic thinking demonstrates both the power of animism and the fragility of boundaries (the door of the fridge, as well as the skin around her body).

Some authors have proposed theories as to why boundary problems may affect girls more often than boys. Raphael-Leff (1986) describes anorectics as women who have never successfully made the crucial early distinction between themselves and their mothers. She suggests that a mother, who herself cannot come to terms with separateness, may blur the boundaries between herself and her baby, resisting the process of differentiation. Especially at risk from this behaviour may be female babies, who are 'symbolically' interchangeable. Later in life such a daughter may demarcate boundaries by claiming strict control over what goes in and comes out of her bodily orifices.

The sense of having a continuous, unchanging body image, with secure boundaries, is uncommon amongst patients with eating disorders. For them, body boundaries are easily changed or lost. Peto (1959) describes an 18-year-old anorectic girl, who, whilst in analysis, felt her body become jelly-like, even liquid. She fantasized that the analyst's body softened too and penetrated or merged with hers in a sort of whirlpool. Peto explains this phenomenon as representing the reappearance of a very early body image – the archaic body image – a structure which is experienced as vague and fluid, of constantly changing form and consistency. This early body image depends, like an embryo, upon physiological factors such as temperature and a sense of body movements. It enables the infant to 'contact and engulf or penetrate mother, fuse with her, to make her part of his own body' (Peto 1959).

This is reminiscent of the 'oceanic feelings' described by Freud, in which the ego merges with the universe; everything outside is at the same time inside: 'The unconscious is that immortal sea which brought us hither, intimations of which are given in moments of oceanic feelings, one sea of energy or instinct, embracing all, in one mystical or symbolic body' (Freud 1985).

These concepts are crucial to the fantasized power to engulf, devour, cannibalize the mother, which will be explored in the next chapter. The experience of fusion, described here, may contain an impression of unrestrained omnipotence, that is, the magical power to engulf. Sylvia Plath (1963) describes her longing for fusion:

As from a star, I saw, coldly and soberly the separateness of everything. Felt the wall of my skin, I am I. That stone is a stone. My beautiful fusion with the things of the world was over.

Both of these quotations refer to the development of the boundary between the self and the external world. Although concepts relating to boundaries may be culturally determined and constructed, individuals have a unique conception of inner and outer space in relation to the body. The thin divide is the body of the skin. In studies of early infant development, Bick (1968) describes how the baby is held together phychically by the experience of a 'second skin'. This is the notion of a body boundary which is holding the infant together, literally like a skin. The infant develops means by which he/she can maintain the sense of this skin remaining intact, since a hole is equivalent to psychic disintegration and must be defended against at all costs. The defences, such as projection and introjection, which are in place at the earliest stages of infant development, were first described by Klein (1961a). These concepts presuppose an even earlier notion of the existence of the organism within its boundaries than the Freudian model of the boundary between the ego and the id. Both, however, are maintained and fortified by the individual's use of defence mechanisms.

Later analysts have questioned the idea of such early boundary formation. For Winnicott (1980), the fundamental boundary is that between 'me and not me', which he suggests corresponds not only to the skin of the body but also to the infant's awareness of the self in relation to the reality of another – either mother or an external, usually loved, object. This creates a fundamental or transitional space where growth occurs and where self and inner psychic reality begin to develop. Although the perception of inner and outer spaces is largely a mental construction, it can also be seen to derive from the language of the body. Winnicott describes how the infant will become attached to a transitional object in order to negotiate the sense of 'me and not me' and the transitional space between mother and self. The concept of transitional phenomena 'is a baby who wants to eat . . . sometimes . . . it is a malignant other, who wishes to eat me . . . it occupies the space between where I end and the other . . . begins' (Winnicott 1980). Freud also suggests that this perception of inner and outer spaces can be related to the language of the oral instinctual impulses, in that the individual has the concept, 'I should like to eat this [take it into myself]', or 'I should like to spit that out'; that is, 'It shall be inside or outside me'. Freud explains that the original pleasure ego wants to introject into itself all that is good, and to eject from itself all that is bad.

From a psychological perspective, Piaget (1929) examines the lack of boundary existing between subject and object or inside and outside. He shows that the child's experience is a continuum of consciousness. Whatever impinges upon the child's senses is identified with the attendant organization of his/her own interior. This experience of continuity is emphasized by the relationship with the mother, who responds to or even anticipates the infant's requirements, thereby symbolically creating a unit between the two, with no idea of dissociation.

How this lack of dissociation relates particularly to patients with eating disorders is described by Boris:

> The anorectic does not have a good set of boundaries. Just as food-hunger is a ruse, the flames of which are fanned to obscure object-hunger, so food itself is a counterfeit substance to substitute for a longing for fusion . . . for being held in body and mind.
>
> (Boris 1984)

For anorectics, the pull towards a state of fusion is opposed by a pull towards separation, in an attempt to avoid being engulfed. An intermediate position is created within a 'transitional space'. This acts like a buffer, a neutral zone between two bodies. The anorectic fails to negotiate herself within this neutral zone and therefore within this space between fusion and separation. As a result of this lack of separateness, she creates for herself an 'in-myself space'. Like the infant, she envies the mother's breast, and so tries to deny its existence. In other words, envy results from the realization of separateness even though she attempts to deny it. However, the alternative to separation is fusion, which is even more dangerous. Figure 4.3 portrays how one patient experienced the lack of difference between her and her mother.

Fears of letting in the mother are closely associated with the feeling that she can easily become part of the 'in-myself space', and so will be assimilated. The anorectic has therefore to deal with both her terror and her longing for this. The envy fuels her wish to deny the mother her separateness but this is combined with the longing to be fused or at one with her. This causes the anorectic to destroy her own sense of separateness and in turn leads to the feeling of being enslaved by another.

The inner space created and guarded by the anorectic affords her a sense of survival. There is no transitional space for her. She lives (metaphorically) without a skin. For her, the question is how to let in food, yet not let it become *part of her*. Food has the ability to penetrate the 'of-me' boundary and to reach the very core of her self. This can be linked directly to her experience with her mother and the underlying anxiety about the boundaries and space between them.

The intake of food involves crossing the boundary from outside to inside. Food, which crosses this boundary produces a crisis. It may easily cross the compensatory inner space that the patient has created for herself as a 'me/not-me' buffer; it may cross the space between 'in-me' and 'of-me'. This concept enables us to understand further how food is considered dangerous, since, through assimilation, it can become part of 'myself'. Particular forms of eating behaviour, such as repeated chewing, could be seen as an attempt to slow down this process.

Food represents a mixture of psychic danger and reassurance. It exists both in the outer world and within the body but may exercise its power, perhaps of a sadistic nature, from inside the body. Klein (1961a) believes that sadistic fantasies directed against the inside of the mother's body constitute the first and most basic relation to the

Figure 4.3

outside world and to reality. The interior of her body not only becomes the representative of her whole person as an object but also symbolizes the external world.

Winnicott (1980) focuses instead on the experience of an inter-face, a boundary or a place of contact, in establishing a sense of reality. He develops the concept of the 'good enough mother' who allows the child to fuse his/her pre-disposition to hallucinate a good situation with the earliest sensations of that actual experience. In other words, the child oscillates between the illusion of union and the fact of contact, which perhaps serves to describe the child's discovery of 'me' and 'you'. The forms in which these unions or contacts occur may vary, although there is a common factor in the destruction or loss of discrimination and interface. This may be seen in terms of the unconscious union with the marvellous (or the atrocious) inner object, in which an obliteration of inner boundaries occurs, particularly between the ego and the incorporated object.

The desire for an obliteration of the inner–outer boundary, for a transcendental state, exists powerfully in many forms. R. D. Laing (1960) discusses the schizoid person in a way that is relevant to many patients with eating disorders:

> The self then seeks by being unembodied to transcend the world and hence to be safe. But a self is liable to develop which feels it is outside all experience and activity. It becomes a vacuum. Everything is there, outside; nothing is here, inside. Moreover, the constant dread of all that is there, of being overwhelmed, is potentiated . . . by the need to keep the world at bay . . . giving in to this weakness [of longing for participation] . . . the individual fears that his vacuum will be obliterated, that he will be engulfed or otherwise lose his identity, which has come to be equated with the maintenance of the transcendence of the self even though this is a transendence in a void.

> (Laing 1960)

Chapter 5

Eating and the body and eating the body

DINAH	'Where did I live before I was born? I don't know.'
MOTHER	'In my tummy.'
DINAH	'And did you eat me up?'
MOTHER	'No.'
DINAH	'And what did I eat?'
MOTHER	'Some of my food, because you were in my tummy.'

(Davidson and Fay 1972)

The child's earliest fantasies originate in the feeding situation. By feeding, the child makes the mother part of him/herself. The mouth is not only the means of physical survival but also the centre of the infant's emotional life. The feeding situation provides the earliest experience of the 'give and take' of human relationships. The pleasure of sucking, biting and taking into oneself are ever-present with food and within relationships. Adult sexual behaviour may involve kissing or biting – a recapitulation of the early pleasures of the mouth.

At this early level of sensation, the equation between food and the mother is natural. She is there literally to be eaten from, a continuing source of physical and emotional fulfilment. The infant is at times consumed by his/her own devouring wishes: to possess the mother, to have her inside, to eat her up. At this stage it seems possible for only one person to exist, the logic of which suggests that either the baby possesses the mother or the mother possesses the baby.

There is an intermingling of food, mother-and-baby's body, devouring wishes, life and death: the devourer and the devoured become fused. At the first hint of the mother having a separate body and existence, there dawns on the baby an intolerable realization that it is the mother who possesses what the baby needs. The infant's growing awareness of his/her dependency on this other person may evoke such envy that it can be managed only by finding some way to possess what is wanted. One such way occurs through fusion.

At stages in our lives we all move along a continuum ranging from a state of isolation to one of fusion. When dominated by either extreme, we are precluded from establishing a sense of self which is not only distinct but also related to the world. We strive paradoxically towards both poles. We balance our conflicting needs for separation and relatedness or for individuation and belonging. The patient with an eating disorder has great difficulty with the concept of relatedness. The symbiotically attached person cannot manage the experience of dependency particularly because he/she does not have a clear delineation between him/herself and the other person. Dependency presupposes a clear distinction between two people, one of whom is dependent upon the other. This in turn is dependent upon the existence of secure ego boundaries. Thus, a kaleidoscopic image begins to appear, in which all of these concepts are interrelated. The lack of an enduring separate sense of the self easily allows the illusion of merging with the other person and this intensifies the threat of being engulfed.

Freud's concept of incorporation has added much to this area. The term refers to the way in which, in fantasy, some object enters the body and is kept inside. This may be simply because it is pleasurable. Alternatively, it may be a way of getting rid of the external item or even of returning to magical ideas, a way of appropriating the object's power and qualities. In the early stages of child development, incorporation of the object is inevitable, since there is no other way to relate to it.

This links very closely to the psychoanalytic use of the term 'cannibalistic'. Freud (1964) writes that the aim of the cannibalistic act is to assure one's identification with (for instance) the father by incorporating part of him. Freud describes these beliefs as originating in the oral stage of development, during which the sexual aim consists of incorporating the object.

There are many examples of cannibalistic thinking (see Figure 5.1). The psychoanalyst Abraham (1979) writes about a patient of his who he describes as having 'a libidinal fixation at the oral or cannibalistic stage'. As a boy the patient had believed that loving somebody was exactly the same as eating something good. He had

Figure 5.1

had a whole range of fantasies about his favourite nurse, having wanted to 'swallow her, skin, hair, clothes and all' (Abraham 1979).

This patient also made conscious links between eating meat and eating human flesh, a theme which I have found to emerge regularly amongst the large number of anorectic patients who are vegetarian (see Figure 5.2). Abraham goes on to describe other patients' cannibalistic fantasies. One involved the wish to bite off the nose or the lobe of the ear or the breast of a young girl of whom the patient was very fond. Abraham considers that these impulses,

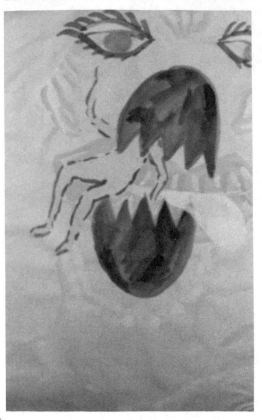

Figure 5.2

rather than having a purely destructive aim, serve quite a different function, namely a 'friendly' saving of the remainder of the person.

This is a fantasy world in which one body may invade another, may devour or swallow up the other, resulting in the annihilation of the self. My impression is that cannibalistic fantasies are fundamentally to do with creating a bodily self. The fragility of the body boundaries of patients with eating disorders means that, for them, closeness or intimacy cannot be distinguished clearly from the threat of being swallowed up by the other person or being overwhelmed by their own devouring wishes to possess and swallow up that person. If two people become too close, only one may survive (see Figure 5.3).

For some patients this situation may result in a type of withdrawal

Figure 5.3

from the world of external relationships and a retreat into a position
of only truly relating to internal figures, or one in which relationships are replaced by a substance, such as drugs or alcohol, or by
their association with food.

The patient uses incorporation and fusion to achieve the desired
intimacy and to experience a particular feeling, such as being
soothed, a state which these patients have extreme difficulty in
creating for themselves. A potential provider of such soothing
sensations cannot be allowed to exist as a real, separate, human
being because this person would not be totally under the patient's

control and would therefore be capable of independent thought which could at any moment exclude the patient. Thus, a substance or a person must be used in such a way that they can be immediately replaced if the need arises, because the patient's life is felt to depend upon what is needed. If the patient feels so incapable of existing were the umbilical cord to be severed, then the ever-present threat that the other person has the power to cut off that lifeline is a threat which cannot be tolerated. It must be evaded in some way.

This is the terrible dilemma facing heroin addicts, who are somehow aware that their dependency upon their dealers is an intolerable state of affairs. A loving partnership is struck up with the actual substance: it is they and the drug against the world. Heroin is their saviour, their one way out of having to face the realities of life which seem to exist in all human relationships, namely the facts of dependency, of potential abandonment, and of fears of literally not being able to survive alone. Heroin is the answer to those brutal facts – until, that is, the harsh reality of addiction dawns. The very drug that seemed to promise always to be their best friend and to save them from the horrors of actual relationships has turned against them. Rather than allowing the addicts to continue to control it, the drug begins to control them, to the extent that they become as enslaved to the drug, as utterly dependent upon its existence, as they might ever have been upon another human being. The drug, however, is without mercy. In this situation there seems to be no way out.

Of course there is a way out, but not whilst the person is actively caught up in the addictive cycle where enslavement banishes any freedom which might be desired. The person desperately wants to feel free from the struggle to survive; free to be able to exist alone without the ever-present threat of dissolution, and therefore free to engage in close relationships, without becoming enslaved or addicted to them.

Whatever substance is used, the more the person is under the influence of intensified separation anxiety and the more he/she is unable to conjure up and to hold on to good caretaking internal objects, the more urgent becomes the impetus towards incorporation and fusion. When it is another person rather than a substance that is used, the threat of destruction to the self, which is inherent in the very object needed to soothe the self, may have to be managed. One way of doing so is by adjusting the interpersonal closeness in order to prevent any relationship from becoming either too close or too distant. Sometimes equilibrium is maintained by spreading the source of gratification amongst many different people, and so not allowing any prolonged intimacy with one person in particular. Another way in which the threat is frequently managed is by becoming involved in a rapid succession of relationships, each doomed almost before it has begun.

The reality for the patient with an eating disorder who is functioning at this level is that she fears that whatever has to be done in order to save her identity will involve her in destroying the very object upon which she feels she depends for her survival. She must face the horror of her own cannibalistic wishes, especially as they are directed towards the very people whom she loves. Her fear interferes with the desired holding–soothing relationship which she so badly needs and which would allow the development of her own sense of self. It is for this reason that the processes of incorporation and fusion actually inhibit the development of self.

Because patients with severe eating disorders lack what is referred to as sufficient 'holding introjects', that is, images of figures who can be called upon internally to look after the self, being alone poses particular problems for them. This level of experience describes much of the borderline level of functioning, in which the patients describe an inner emptiness, a state of 'aloneness'. This is quite different from a feeling of loneliness in which there is some sense of the other who is missing. In some ways loneliness describes the lack of necessary others outside of the individual whilst aloneness describes a lack of internal comforters. The void that is often described is akin to a sense of deadness and meaninglessness which, again, has a different quality from that of depression. When in this particular state, the patient is often driven to some impulsive act, such as bingeing, self-mutilation or shoplifting, or to a variety of other behaviours which serve to bring the person to life again. We shall look much closer at this area of impulsive behaviour in later chapters.

Many authors stress the importance of the role of envy in the wish to consume and possess that which does not belong to the self. However, I should rather emphasize the desire for survival. It seems reasonable that a patient with such an impoverished sense of self might feel compelled to devour what appears to be a strong self and to have it inside herself.

Klein (1961a) describes the infant's early sadistic fantasies as focusing at first on the mother's breast and then gradually extending to the whole of her body. In his/her imagination the child attacks the body, robbing it of everything that it contains and eating it up. When patients with eating disorders permit themselves to speak about their cannibalistic fantasies, they often describe the magical hope of becoming more whole by devouring the other. Their representation of a nebulous self existing in unembodied space, which may be consumed and wiped out like a cloud passing over the sun, contrasts dramatically with their view of the other person who appears 'embodied' and to have a 'self'.

In these patients there is profound confusion with regard to several questions. Who has the desirable bodily substance and who desires it? Where does this bodily substance come from and where does it go? Who owns it, and if one possesses it, is it lost from the other? Is there such a thing as an individual self? We cannot assume that these patients operate with an enduring sense of two separate bodies existing in relationships. Prestage (1976) quotes a piece of writing by an anorectic patient in which she describes first how she imagines that her mother feels towards her and then her own feelings:

> It's a girl. Eat the child, bind the child, claw the child. It is the first, it is your possession. Never let it go. Eat the child.

> I am destroyed and eaten. By the hunger of bitterness and shame. I let this happen because I am rotting inside. I am hiding a fungus not a flower. And daily it eats me, I drank the pollen of greedy rot from the breast, and now I am poisoned.

> (Prestage 1976)

It is possible to understand how the anorectic, by controlling her own needs and appetites, is, in fantasy, also controlling her internal mother. Her fear is not of becoming *like* her mother but of actually *becoming* her mother.

The great difficulty that these patients have in dealing with their hatred and aggression must not be ignored. Very often it is apparent from their histories that their aggressive feelings could not be managed within their families and that they attach tremendous danger to overt expressions of such feelings. It is as if they cannot believe that either they or the person(s) on the receiving end could possibly survive their utterance. The reason for this lies partly in their difficulty in imagining having very strong, angry feelings without having to act upon them or, referring back to an earlier theme, without damage being incurred magically by the mere thought. Some theories suggest that the fear of eating is closely linked to fantasies of having actually killed the hated object during the oral cannibalistic attacks of infancy. This conveys the fear that is associated with such a sense of omnipotence. According to Kleinian theory, aggressive feelings are projected on to the mother, in forms such as images of wicked, devouring witches with long teeth who eat little children, but it was originally the child during the oral stage who wished to devour the mother.

Some writers suggest that the child and later the adult (unconsciously) feels that he/she deserves to be punished for having so greedily 'sucked the breast dry and bitten it to pieces'. Weaning may be experienced as one form of punishment. The mastication of food may at some level put the individual in touch with his/her destructive wishes to bite and devour the mother and so may lead to a rejection of certain fleshy foods.

The link between anger and hunger has been well documented, especially recently by feminist therapists who have described how the socialization of women emphasizes that they are not meant to express their anger overtly. Since the early work of Melanie Klein, the object-relations analysts have much to offer present day understanding of these patients. Guntrip, for example, describes the schizoid condition in relation to hunger:

> when you cannot get what you want from the person you need, instead of getting angry, you may simply go on getting more and more hungry, and full of a sense of painful craving and a longing to get total and complete possession of your love object so you cannot be left to starve.
>
> (Guntrip 1982)

In this way love itself becomes so devouring and so incorporative that it is felt to be very destructive. Guntrip describes the horror of feeling like 'one great mouth wanting to eat everything and everybody'. For many of these patients, therefore, to love someone appears to be like a mutual eating process; taken to extreme, any close human contact may seem to hold the danger of mutual incorporation.

There is a link between these patients' difficulties in sustaining contact and their inability to deal with their own destructiveness. Many fear their own capacity to destroy a good relationship, were it to exist in the first place. Others seem to understand that their capacity to tolerate the very ordinary difficulties that must be faced in any enduring contact with another person is severely curtailed. It may be hampered by their extreme jealousy or possessiveness, which is based upon the belief that the wanted person is equally as incapable as themselves of having more than one person in mind at any time. If the other were to show concern about a third person, this would be regarded as total abandonment. This painful state of affairs may lead to relationships in which the aim is to try either to hold the other person captive or to deny this frenzied wanting of them by distancing. The fear is that their jealousy or, more particularly, their envy or sense of abandonment might cause them to lose control of their violent feelings.

Envy, which may also be evoked when the individual feels loved, may propel her into destructiveness, which is sometimes encapsulated in an attack on food, a violent binge. Such destructive feelings of envy are not induced merely by being loved; they may extend to any person who attempts to reach out in a kind or helpful way. This has great relevance to the therapeutic relationship. For the patient, it is very difficult to accept from, be fed by, someone who is brimming over with things to give; by comparison, the patient feels so empty or perhaps hateful.

These conflicts contribute somewhat to the destructive element within cannibalistic ideas. However, there are many other important dimensions, one of which is the oral component of incorporative ideas. Earlier, we considered the problems posed for these patients as a result of their failure to achieve an enduring sense of separate identity. To understand this we are required to think differently about dependency within such relationships. Usually dependency implies that two separate people exist, either mutually dependent or one dependent upon the other. That is not what occurs, however, in the case of a number of these patients. If, instead, we try to think 'incorporatively', we may appreciate how the individual, rather than being dependent on a separate object/ person outside of her own self boundary, may extend the limits, widening her 'self-boundary circle' in order to include the other person within it. The wanted person is thus scooped up, sucked in and swallowed and made part of the self. In this way all good and wanted things are not allowed to remain separate and in their own space but must be possessed.

What is it that allows most of us to enjoy, say, a Monet exhibition at an art gallery without the frantic urge to own all the paintings and to have them to ourselves at home? If we were to be driven to distraction by the fact that they existed independently of our feelings about them and that they were available for thousands of others to enjoy too, we might choose to go nowhere near the exhibition or perhaps to steal the paintings or even to destroy them, so that no one else could enjoy them.

How does this help us to understand the link between cannibalistic ideas, incorporation and orality? At the earliest stages of development, the period of primal narcissism, the oral zone is all-important because of the total nutritional dependence upon the breast. Since, at this stage, the infant does not differentiate between her mother and herself, the breast is regarded as part of herself and the pleasure gained from absorbing its contents provides supreme narcissistic gratification.

The libido, at this time, is focused on the mouth, on sucking and swallowing. Slightly later, biting is added as an aggressive and sadistic activity. Valued objects, therefore, are those which can be sucked and swallowed. Some writers have proposed the existence of an 'oral character', that is, someone who is unconsciously preoccupied with ways of gratifying the urge to incorporate; someone who may be intent on being close to certain people to be assured of obtaining 'supplies' from them and to guarantee the gratification of dependent fantasies. For some, these incorporative fantasies may take the form of an optimistic expectation but for others there may lurk a suspicion that 'scarcity will prevail' (perhaps linked to the bulimic's need to buy food in bulk quantities). Other patients may perhaps display compensatory generosity, to conceal the hidden avarice that is often described by anorectics who wish to feed others.

Some early theories of anorexia nervosa suggested that food refusal is a defence against oral sadistic and cannibalistic fantasies. Other theories highlighted a different anxiety, namely that self-starvation is a defence against oral impregnation. Freud in 1908 proposed that, to the young child, food may symbolize the paternal phallus which, when ingested, conceives the oedipal baby. Later psychoanalytic concepts have integrated the Freudian original drive conflict model and object relations theory. The anorectic is seen to have unresolved problems in the oral incorporative stage, which have impeded the process of separation and individuation. The anorectic fantasizes the oral incorporation of a bad, over-controlling maternal object, which is then equated with her own

body. Self-starvation is often viewed as the adolescent's attempt to
end the feminization of her body and to minimize the confused and
ambivalent identification with her mother.

The battle to reclaim herself is fought within her own body, which
is partially equated with that of her mother's body. In a powerless,
helpless way, the patient is 'consumed' with and by the mother. The
physical paradox inherent in the appearance of the anorectic's body
is that it is open to invasion. The anorectic physically appears
unable to protect herself and demonstrates by her fragility that
which has led her to feel so helpless and impotent. Thoughts and
feelings are being expressed concretely through the body. There is a
lack of differentiation between what is mental and what is physical.
At the earliest stages of development, one thing commonly stands
for another. Kestenberg (1956) describes how 'the mouth . . . as the
model opening becomes the symbol of all holes of the body. Thus
the vaginal opening becomes endowed with oral representations
stemming from a direct equation with the mouth.'

In order that one thing may be used to represent or symbolize
another, each must be understood to exist in its own right. Otherwise
the two lack space between them and are combined. By understanding what is necessary in order to think symbolically we can
seek to understand what is lacking in patients with eating disorders
and to focus therapeutic work on their difficulties in symbolic
functioning. With this in mind it is essential to have an idea of
what food means for the patient with an eating disorder. For example, if food represents taking something in from the mother, when
there is no functioning with symbolic thinking, then it may be
experienced as the actual incorporation of the mother.

For all people, food may at times symbolize comfort, or unobtain-
able love. It may be used as an expression of rage or as a substitute
for sexual gratification. In some cases, food may symbolize the wish
to have a penis, or to be pregnant. The images we use in everyday
language are rich in symbols of food and feeding: for example,
bitter, sweet, acid, biting, mincing one's words, snapping his head
off, holding one's tongue. The language of relationships has even
more of this imagery: push down one's throat, spoon-fed, swallow
something whole, digest ideas, chew things over, take things in,
drink in or lap up something, get one's teeth into something, starved
of love, hungry for knowledge, consumed with envy, fed up. The list
is endless. Metaphors, such as keeping something/someone alive
inside, although understandable through the use of concepts such as

internalization or incorporation, may intrinsically be bound up with the nature of eating. Marion, the heroine in Margaret Atwood's *The Edible Woman*, provides an example of the way in which food can become endowed with human qualities, in more than a symbolic fashion:

> She cut into the [pink heart-shaped] cake. She was surprised to find that it was pink in the inside too. She put a forkful into her mouth and chewed slowly. It felt spongy and cellular against her tongue, like the bursting of thousands of tiny lungs. She shuddered and spat the cake out into her napkin.
>
> (Atwood 1980)

Marion demonstrates some degree of identification with this inanimate object, and so is repelled by the cannibalistic inference.

In another scene, Marion carries out a final act of self-assertion. She bakes a cake which is shaped and decorated like the body of a woman:

> The cake looked peculiar with only a mouth and no hair or eyes. She drew a nose and two large eyes [with chocolate icing] to which she appended many eyelashes and two eyebrows, . . . For emphasis she made a line demarcating one leg from the other, and similar lines to separate the arms from the body. The hair took longer, it involved masses of intricate baroque scrolls and swirls, . . . Her creation gazed up at her . . . 'You look delicious', she told her, 'very appetising . . . that's what you get for being food'. Her [the cake's] fate had been decided.
>
> (Atwood 1980)

Marion's pity for this cake-woman (to do with her identification with it) does not prevent her from presenting it to a horrified Peter, and saying, 'you've been trying to destroy me, haven't you . . . you've been trying to assimilate me, but I've made you a substitute . . . I'll get you a fork . . .' (1980). Her sense of literally being devoured and swallowed up is powerfully portrayed in this scene in which food has become animated and a danger to her.

Food being endowed with animism occurs quite frequently in the fantasies of patients with eating disorders and is related to their fears concerning their own cannibalistic impulses. Freud's understanding of animism was based on the process of projection, in which our representation of the external world comes about by placing our internal perceptions outside. (Whether this mechanism presupposes some awareness of an internal and external divide is worth debating but cannot be followed up here.) Piaget's understanding of the development of animistic modes of thinking can be linked to food and eating. At the earliest stage of development there is confusion between the self and other objects and the infant attempts to exert magical activity over reality. He/she is at first 'at one' with the mother's breast, unaware of the other's existence, and experiences by wish or hallucination (or by good timing) the desired satisfaction.

Patients with eating disorders similarly wish to be able to satisfy their own hungers; they too experience confusion between themselves and others and have great difficulty in recognizing feelings which originate from within their own bodies. Eating is separated from the satisfaction of hunger and becomes instead a means by which they may control the food.

Why do these patients feel the need to exert such influence over not only their bodies but also the food they eat? According to Klein (1961b), during the process of feeding, the baby feels that he/she takes into him/herself the nourishing function of the mother (Klein terms this the 'good breast'), which is then capable of living inside him/her and fulfilling his/her needs. This fantasy, Klein suggests, persists throughout life. When the baby feels angry or frustrated, however, this experience is transformed into that of having something bad pushed into him/her and it provokes great anxiety lest this object should attack him/her from within. The infant's response, therefore, is to push or project the bad object out of his/her body into the external world. Davidson and Fay (1972) describe young Harry, who played a game of swallowing his foster-mother, saying triumphantly, 'now you can't talk'. She was thus silenced until he had ejected her, which he did with a realistic vomiting noise. Harry was sick when he was angry. His analyst interpreted this as Harry having to get rid of the bad deserting mother, who was persecuting him from the inside and making him feel angry. When the mother is experienced as bad she must not be kept inside. When she is good, however, she may yet be damaged, in the child's imagination, by his/her very wish to swallow her greedily.

Abraham (1979) describes a melancholic patient who refused to eat:

> He behaves as though complete abstention from food could alone keep him from carrying out his repressed impulses. At the same

time he threatens himself with that punishment which is alone
fitting for his unconscious cannibalistic impulses – death by
starvation.

(Abraham 1979)

The bulimic's desire to consume large quantities of food may be
equated with taking in the mother. However, if it (she) is devoured,
it (she) may retaliate, and so the desire to incorporate the object, the
'cannibalistic desire', meets powerful internal resistance. The practice of buying or possessing large quantities of food may partially
fulfil the desire (by reducing the anxiety of dying of hunger) but the
need to abstain from eating it, or else to vomit it up, serves to
perpetuate the sense of starvation. Food itself thereby becomes the
object of conflict by virtue of its role as the mother-substitute.

A Kleinian perspective would suggest that the reason why the
internalized breast (or that which is substituted for the breast) might
attack or want retribution is that it has been robbed by the infant. It
therefore becomes dangerous and hostile. Fears of taking from (or
taking in) the mother may underlie later difficulties with eating.
Defences that are developed by the child against his/her other
experience of greed for the breast may result in the child equating
greed with robbing. This results in the fear of retaliation or biting
back from the object/breast.

The mother is therefore associated not only with good things but
also with fantasies of danger, separation and terrible destruction.
The infant's own destructiveness is demonstrated by such feelings
as wanting to tear the good body content from her. The mother's
food may thus be viewed as poisonous, owing to the infant's own
attacks upon her. These attacks may be experienced through the
bodily functions of urinating and defecating. There is therefore a
fantasy of mutual attack and destruction in relation to eating.

Food itself may become persecutory. Davidson and Fay (1972)
describe the way in which a child's greed affects his perception of
food: 'George would selfishly grab at his food and rob others of
theirs. When accused of being greedy, he became disgusted by his
food, and began calling his runner beans crawling green snakes.'
Similarly an anorectic patient, having painted a picture of a large
plate of spaghetti, was embarrassed that I should think that she
might eat as much as that. She began to make associations to the
food itself: the spaghetti could climb off the plate and wrap itself

around her throat to suffocate her. The food had taken on the power to inhibit her eating that she had at first located in me.

The animation of food, together with cannibalistic ideas, appears frequently in mythology and fairy tales. There are near-universal taboos upon the members of any primary group killing and eating each other. In mythology imagery of the mother is associated in almost equal measures with 'beatitude and danger, birth and death, the nourishing breast and tearing claws of the ogress' (Campbell 1929). Fearful 'she-monsters' often destroy men by sucking, swallowing or eating them. Scylla, the six-headed monster, seized and swallowed sailors, plucking them from those ships which had managed to escape from being swallowed up by the whirlpool of Charybdis. The anthropologist Malinowski was told by the Trobriand islanders of an island inhabited only by naked women who had insatiable desires and who devoured stranded sailors.

Cannibalistic tales, especially of ogresses, exist in many lands and cultures. Campbell (1929) describes the fairy tale witch (well known from the tale 'Hansel and Gretel') who lives in a candy house which would be nice to eat. She invites children inside, only because she wants to eat them. Campbell suggests that, on the mythological level, the archetype is elevated into a cosmic symbol in such cannibal – mother goddesses as Kâlî, 'the black one' of the Hindu religion. She is the consumer of the wicked dead, the female mouth, the belly of hell, who is represented with her long tongue lolling out, ready to 'lick up' her children. Simultaneously, however, she is the goddess Annapurna (meaning 'abundance of food'). Similar images are the Egyptian Isis, with her son Horus at her breast, and the Babylonian Ishtar, nursing the moon-god.

The instinct for survival underlies many cannibalistic myths and not only women are assigned this role. An ancient legend tells of Saturn, who devoured his children because it was foretold that otherwise they would devour him. This illustrates the theme of 'eat or be eaten'. Some images are even more malevolent. Davidson and Fay (1972) relate the Russian fairy story, 'The Witch Baby'. This child's beauty is marred by her black iron teeth, which betray her wicked greed. She grows and grows, filling the whole house. Eventually, having devoured both her parents, she sits sucking her thumb and muttering: 'Eaten the father, eaten the mother, and now to eat the little brother' (1972).

An important aspect of cannibalistic fantasies is the notion of fusion or becoming part of the other person. This theme abounds throughout fairy tales, myths and religion: in the Eucharist, for example, or in the marriage feast, which contains the idea of the bride and bridegroom becoming one flesh, incorporating each other by the act of eating.

The belief, stated in Freud (1960), that incorporating parts of a person's body through the act of eating enables one to acquire qualities possessed by that person leads, in some circumstances, to precautions and restrictions of a magical nature. A pregnant woman, for example, may avoid eating the flesh of certain animals for fear of passing on any of their undesirable qualities to the unborn child.

As we have seen, there is a relationship between animate and inanimate, between human and animal flesh, and between the fear of and the desire for being engulfed. All of these elements are associated with cannibalistic ideas.

Chapter 6

Body boundaries with relation to art

In the following chapters I hope to show how my work as an art therapist has developed along certain lines, particularly in connection with the concepts surrounding psychic cannibalism which have been expressed in the art therapy setting.

Within that setting, tangible boundaries are defined by the materials themselves. The physical act of creating a painting provides definition. The painter is acting in relation to some thing which is not of her own body, a separate entity. The very business of painting allows for and even encourages movement between the recognition of separateness in relation to the object and the act of merging with it.

Being 'in relation to' an object should not be overlooked here. Many patients, when describing the stages leading up to a binge or some other destructive behaviour, are aware of an increasing anxiety which is often associated with a feeling of aimlessness. There is a sense of impending danger which has something to do with the dissolution of their personality. I have come to make sense of such descriptions in terms of a loss of connectedness or relatedness, in just the way that a balloon, whose string has been cut, is at the mercy of the wind. Thus, it is easy to understand how therapeutic it is for someone in this state of mind to engage in a purposeful activity which serves to reconnect her to something or to someone.

The painted images may appear to be undefined and without boundaries, and yet they are contained within the limits of the frame, that is, the edge of the paper. Art may be seen to provide not only a means to explore boundary issues but also an appropriate language for this to take place.

The artistic process, which involves the use of creative imagination, necessitates a sense of expansion of the ego boundaries.

However, contact with the ego core is retained (unlike in dreams, which also involve primary process manipulations of time and space). The imagination, which is in essence the formation of mental representations, may of course be used creatively or regressively. This expansion of boundaries of inner and outer awareness may be experienced with an aesthetic, religious or empathic feeling. All are associated with temporary fusion and a degree of loss of differentiation.

We constantly fluctuate between a perception of the internal world and that of the external; in the art process, however, this becomes very clear. The painter steps back from his/her canvas to gain perspective and then goes closer to 'create illusion', using space to facilitate this. At certain moments the onlooker feels at one with the work of art that he/she is looking at; it no longer remains outside of him/herself.

Rose (1963) describes the way in which an amateur female artist (who was also a patient of his) thickened her canvasses with paint, expressing the need to reinforce her 'stimulus barrier'. This raises important questions as to whether the thickening of the barrier referred to her own body, in an attempt to create a more definite boundary for herself, to the body of the therapist, or to the object (the canvas) between the two of them.

Patients with eating disorders very often use a wide variety of means to create boundaries. Anorectics, faced with a large expanse of paper, might use words, written across a small picture either as a title or an explanation, to provide definition. To people who have such limited freedom of expression, words feel more 'boundaried'. One bulimic patient, when painting a self-portrait, emphasized the boundary around her body, in effect creating extra thickening. When discussing why she had done this, she associated it with her desire to know where she 'began and ended', where her limits were. Her bulimia appeared to provide a concrete body boundary for her, and hence an identity (see Figure 6.1).

Another bulimic patient reacted strongly to my suggestion that she use a large sheet of paper, placed under the sheet on which she was working, to provide her with an extra boundary. She was distressed by the marks that she frequently made over the edges of the original paper. Although she had accepted the suggestion, she proceeded to redefine her own, very much larger, boundary by sticking numerous large sheets together on which to place her expanding work. What became apparent in discussion was her

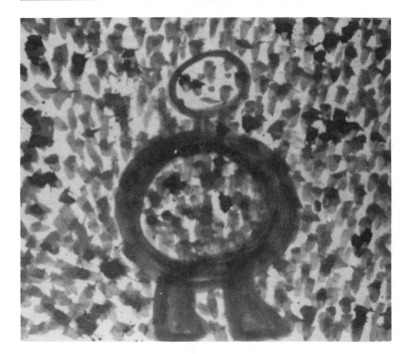

Figure 6.1

panic at my proposed limitation of her space, that is my attempt
to create a boundary for her. The issue of space and territory was
thus brought, through the art object, into our relationship.

For these patients, boundaries are needed not only to define
themselves but also to keep others out, since the potential for
intrusion or invasion is felt to be great. A patient with bulimia
painted a portrait of herself as a 'peeled body', with no skin (see
Figure 6.2). She described herself as raw and in terrible pain
because everything, including my words, hit her body sharply.
She appeared to experience herself as having no protective skin,
nothing to contain or shield her. For her, bingeing temporarily
'healed the rawness'. The physical sensation of fullness seemed to
give her some sense of boundary, and therefore containment, rather
like a satisfied infant after feeding. She produced many paintings of
parts of her body, particularly the stomach, with which she associated ideas of being contained. The stomach might have belonged
to her, or to me, or to anyone; it merely existed as an object for

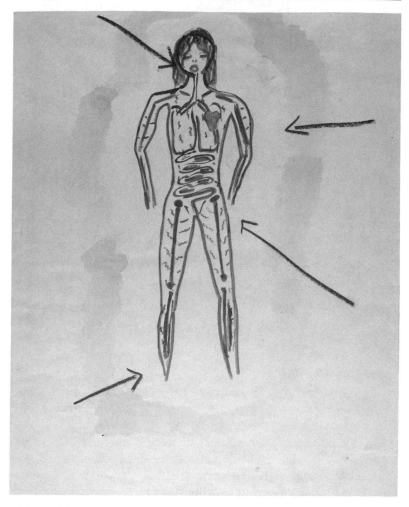

Figure 6.2

containing. Her inability to relate to me as a whole person meant that, for her, I was ineffectual as a symbolic container. During our sessions I would experience her as using me like food, rather than relating to me; she would try to suck me dry. As with other border-line psychotic patients, she had severe distortions in the concept not only of her own body and its parts but also of her relationship to the bodies of others.

Pankow (1961) describes the state of a schizophrenic: 'He is everywhere . . . There is no difference between inside and outside.' She describes the relationship that exists *between* bodies, which contain parts. If there has never 'been a separation between mother and daughter, both constitute one being' (Pankow 1961). One of Pankow's patients brought her a clay statue called the 'flower man'. The body had no head, no neck and no arms. The stomach was in the form of two immense petals, which were open. The most important factor, Pankow notes, was the loss of boundary between the inside and the outside of the figure's body. The initial aim of therapy was to help this patient to use the materials in order to create the body that had been lost; to create a body image. Once a sense of body image begins to be created, this has the fuction of being able to recognize the *external outline*: 'The moment [a patient] is able to distinguish inside from outside, . . . the patient theoretically can be relieved of schizophrenia.' The recognition of the external outline 'leads the patient to understand that a container has a content. For example, that the inside of his body belongs to him as a person' (Pankow 1961).

Although this work was carried out in relation to psychotic patients, I believe that much of the level of functioning of patients with severe eating disorders is of a borderline psychotic quality, particularly with reference to their sense of body boundaries. To seek to understand the dynamics of anorexia, for example, only in terms of a weight phobia is to miss the fundamental boundary issue entirely.

Because these concepts involve a level of functioning that is in part pre-verbal, the use of speech or language to express or discuss these ideas is limited. For example, how can we make sense of the descriptions of pictures or images that are made which concern states of fusion or non-separateness? The original experience, occurring in early infancy, obviously carried no words with it, and so any words and concepts which are utilized now were acquired at a much later stage. Arieti (1976) suggests that either retrospective falsification may occur or, more likely, the memory consists more of a conserving of visual images or 'endocepts' which are translated into words congruous with the person's present level of understanding.

To lose one's sense of self in expansion is the experience of temporarily giving up the discriminating ego, which stands apart and tries to see things objectively. This can be enhancing or

protective and such an 'out-of-body experience' is described by the
French poet Jean Cayrol:

> The prisoner was never present in the place where he was beaten,
> in the place where he was fed, or where he worked . . . even
> torture could be surmounted. When a man was beaten in a
> concentration camp, he sacrificed his body, which became no
> more than garbage - in effect the body was denied. Man can,
> therefore, deny the body that is being whipped and save himself
> by transposition into another world.
>
> (Jean Cayrol, quoted in Pankow 1981).

Pankow attempts to show how, in psychotic states, patients utilize
the possibility of living outside the body. Without a sense of body,
however, there is also little sense of personal identity. For some
patients this may be a temporary defence or refuge but for those
with severe eating disorders, who have such poor body boundaries,
it may necessitate a constant control of potential chaos.

This issue needs to be addressed within the art therapy setting. It
may present itself in various forms. During one session a bulimic
patient was very distressed at her inability to 'do anything'. She
sat and cried over her paper for some time. As in verbal therapy,
the therapist may on occasion feel it appropriate to 'lend words'
and/or suggest actions to the patient to enable her to give some
form to her experience and to communicate this in some way. This
patient seemed so uncontained as not to have the form in which to
communicate interpersonally. I suggested that she cut out body
parts and so form a body. The activity of cutting out seemed to
serve as a distinguishing boundary for her. While creating something separate from herself, she was also in the process of
differentiating herself from it. After this she was able to paint
an image of her body shape which released feelings about her
confusion over her identity. She was unsure as to whether the
person she had painted was herself or her mother. She and her
mother would wear similar clothes and make-up. They were 'best
friends'. However her mother seemed less able to act as an
emotional container for her, being always in competition and
closely identified with her.

For many patients, the identification with their mothers is an
important aspect of their boundary formation and also relates to
their cannibalistic ideas. Fairbairn (1952) drew attention to the
importance of identification in patients, who have a marked

'infantile dependence'. Guntrip (1982) takes up Fairbairn's suggestion that these patients have strong tendencies towards oral incorporation of the love object, the breast–mother. He describes a
feeling of oneness with the mother inside the womb, which pre-
cedes the more active characteristic of oral incorporation.

Imagery of wombs, or containers of some sort, appears frequently
in the artwork of patients with eating disorders and is accompanied
by associations of being passively fed (see Figure 6.3). The desire is
not so much to be inside the mother but to be at one with her. This is
often demonstrated too within the therapeutic relationship, where
patients hope that their thoughts or needs will be known by me,

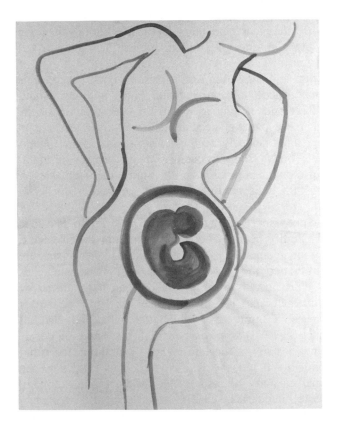

Figure 6.3

magically, without their having taken any active part in communicating them.

Other images, such as those to do with permeability, are more subtle. Paintings of vaginas, fabric or leaking roofs are examples of patients' associations with 'things getting in or out' or with something not being strong enough to keep an object in or out. These types of images seem to concern the potential danger involved in two objects/bodies being in contact or interacting with each other. The danger lies in the breaking down of body boundaries and in the potential for being swallowed up, that is, psychic cannibalism. The fear of losing oneself in another person is also highlighted by the particular anxieties of anorectic patients when faced with blank sheets of paper. Anxieties about the empty space are described as creating feelings of 'nothingness'. This may be understood in terms of the need of these patients to have something by which to be defined. Similarly they describe fears of disintegrating whenever they are alone. In the absence of a defining object their sense of self is highly precarious.

The dissolution of body boundaries also serves to create a different 'mental space', a transcendental place without boundaries, as a means of not having to live within the confines of the body. Although these patients need to feel contained, or held in some way, they simultaneously need to exist outside of the (potentially) containing body. They frequently create images of themselves on top of mountains or clouds, illustrating their fantasies of being up amongst the gods, beyond the dictates of bodily needs and limitations.

Anorectics do not want 'treatment'. They do not want to be forced into a world of bodily needs. The bulimic has not found such a successful way of maintaining this position, as she repeatedly attempts to empty her body of its feelings and then re-engages with her body. This process of emptying out can be explored by her use of the art materials. The material itself can provide part of the concrete space, a frame over which the individual has full control. Winnicott's (1980) work on potential space and the development of boundaries shows the importance of attaining the capacity to be alone in the presence of another. This relates to the mother's original capacity to respect the child's space, allowing the latter to create boundaries, separate from her own. The experience can be achieved during the activity of painting, in the presence of an unobtrusive therapist who has created space for that purpose.

In this setting, issues of self and other-relatedness can be explored through image-making.

It is important to recognize what the image says about boundaries. Some images convey their message more clearly than others. Locked doors, high walls or closed curtains not only refer to the individual hiding inside but also serve as means of protection. As a therapist I understand these messages to be direct communications to me to 'keep out': whatever these patients 'allow in' has to be fully under their control. This explains the self-disgust and great fear that are associated with out-of-control binges.

Bulimic patients frequently describe their fantasies of eating the paint, or perhaps of smearing it over themselves, whilst using it. Similarly, they associate their work with having 'vomited' something out. In the very act of dealing with the art materials, they appear to be bringing alive the issues of inner and outer, of external substances moving in and out of the body boundary. The art therapist can utilize this process to therapeutic effect. Rather than merely providing a setting in which the constant repetition of symptomatic behaviour may be acted out, he/she can offer 'a setting with a difference' in terms both of materials used and of how space, boundaries and communications, used concretely and interpersonally, are dealt with.

Bulimics often create 'smear' or 'mess' paintings, using finger paints or dollops of thick poster paint, and describe the revulsion that they felt during the production of such images. Some describe these as being the spilling out of their body contents – blood, vomit or faeces – on to and over the paper. One patient, after an exhausting session during which she used vast amounts of paper, paints and space, hung her heavy, torn, distorted painting on the wall. Taking hold of my hand she led me some distance from the painting and, pointing to it, said, 'That's me over there – just spilling out, all disgusting.' When I asked her if she also felt that she was standing there next to me, she replied, 'Actually, I don't feel like I'm here at all. It's really nice.' This patient (like many multi-impulsive bulimics) had also severely abused alcohol and drugs. By means of the painting it seemed that she had recreated the oblivion that drugs can induce, the state of separateness from her own body. The aim of such behaviour is, I believe, not merely to escape the confines of the body but also to achieve a state of fusion with the mother or with all things – the oceanic experience that Freud described (see Chapter 4).

This patient's inability to live in her body, with all of its disturbing contents and feelings, was very apparent. When she had got rid of ('vomited up') her intolerable self, she achieved the semi-dissociated state in which she was free to do something that was highly uncharacteristic of her: she held my hand. It became clear to her that part of what was involved in splitting off or getting rid of parts of herself was her fearful inability to tolerate and contain in her own body different, conflicting and threatening parts of herself, many of which she had tried to disown in numerous ways.

Pankow (1976) talks of helping her psychotic patients to recognize the boundaries of their bodies. She suggests that, in order for them to experience and accept material which can be exchanged symbolically with others, they first have to create a form, a container, with dynamic properties, namely a bounded body image. In Pankow's 'dynamic structurization' therapy, the initial vehicle for devising this basic, personal form is the patient's creation of dynamic images (drawings or sculptures in clay). These reveal to the therapist the way in which the patient lives in his/her own body. Once an intermediary form/container exists in the therapeutic setting, the patient can gradually begin to feel the relationship between form and content and to experience this dialect, which does not exist in a 'formless', fragmented state. These ideas can be taken only so far with regard to patients with severe eating disorders because they appear to be far more 'embodied' than Pankow's schizophrenic patients, even though they may deal with their bodies in an utterly mechanistic and concrete fashion.

The relationship between form and content is also discussed by Winnicott (1980). He suggests that content is meaningless without form and, with relevance to the practice of art therapy, that spontaneity makes sense only in a controlled setting. Thus, the frequent images of unboundedness (vast seas, skies, abstractions without definable forms) which occur in the painting of patients with eating disorders can be of value therapeutically only because they are contained within some external structure: first the paper; next, the room; and then the individual's relationship with the therapist. Images which involve switching between creating boundaries and then destroying them can be 'held' by the conscious recognition of what the individual is doing. 'Art provides a medium between the self-created world and external reality – and this medium is considered to be essential for the development of object relationships'(Milner 1952).

Through the art-making process, the individual can objectively explore her personal boundaries by creating boundaries in the external world and by dealing with boundaries in space. A personal 'boundary' actually bears little relation to reality. Originally, the ego includes everything within its boundary and only later does it detach itself from the external world. The language which is used, such as 'keeping someone alive inside', involves the concept of introjection and denies the reality of separate body boundaries. In accepting these concepts, one temporarily suspends the reality principle.

Klein (1961a) suggests that, through the mechanisms of introjection and projection, the infant's 'object' can be defined as what is inside or outside his/her own body. Even whilst outside, however, the 'object' is still part of him/herself, since it has been 'spat out'. Thus, body boundaries are blurred. Both art and psychoanalysis can provide a framework within which a definition and a safe expansion of ego boundaries may occur. If expansion happens without retaining contact with the ego core, it may be only an apparent expansion. There is little possibility of assimilation and growth, only of substitution. This is of relevance to the art therapist, whose patients may frequently substitute the art activity for their other impulsive means of expression. At these times, the therapist must help these patients to recognize their core ego.

By stimulating the imagination, art induces an external expansion and offers itself as a new skin, a mirror, a mask or a body image for the observer (and/or creator) to try for size. The actual activity involves choosing lines and shapes, giving shape and form to an image; in other words, the artist is creating boundaries for herself. These self-boundaries may not then be confused with those of another person. The patient is working in a territory over which she has full control, unlike that of her own body.

The act of being separate from and then merging with the painting provides an experience of moving to and from the external–internal world. Unlike the experience within an intimate, interpersonal relationship, the painting does not engulf the individual but provides the possibility of acting on an external reality as well as exploring the physical sense of the person's own body.

When very distressed patients harm themselves, perhaps by banging their heads repeatedly against a wall, what is it that they are actually doing? In part, they may be creating a sense of an external boundary, a physical limit to themselves. They may describe this as making themselves feel 'real' (as people often say about cutting their wrists) but this of course presupposes a prior sense of unreality, not only of an hysterical, dissociative sort but also arising from an *out-of-body* experience. The act of painting similarly imposes physical limitations which produce an external boundary. Patients with poor boundaries have a great need for external limits to contain them. For patients with eating disorders these external boundaries may be constructed from the magical ideas surrounding the intake of food. As long as food is kept *outside*, nothing can impinge and so potentially damage from the *inside*. Inside and outside have to be kept securely controlled.

Chapter 7

Art and psychic cannibalism

The discussion in Chapter 6 of the relationship between the art process and body boundaries is essential to understanding the nature of the cannibalistic imagery which so frequently occurs.

In one directed art exercise, a bulimic and an anorectic patient paired up to paint together. What occurred between them, highlighted by the process within the activity, was fundamental to both patients' ways of relating to others. The anorectic patient (A) was unable, in the presence of the bulimic patient (B), to create any independent images. She feared a violent retaliation by B if she were to do so. She felt that to 'be herself' would provoke B into attacking her; instead she chose constantly to appease B (who did not require appeasement) by following her work around the paper, adding to and elaborating on B's images. She felt that B's capacity to 'swallow her up' on the page was so strong that her best line of defence was 'not to be there', so that B could have nothing to devour except the empty space. Patient B, on the other hand, was frightened by the strength of her own feelings and by her capacity to dominate A. Rather than feeling appeased, when A expressed her reason for chasing B around the paper, B explained how the very thing from which A had been attempting to protect herself (namely, being swallowed up) had in fact been her own sentiment. A's protestations that she feared being devoured by B had actually created a situation in which *B* felt that she was swallowed up.

A similar dynamic is frequently seen in the families of anorectics where the mother ends up feeling that she is not allowed any space by her anorectic daughter. The invasion and intrusion which the anorectic fears and against which she defends herself so powerfully, so as not to take in anything, is acted out in reverse. By carefully interpreting this situation, patient A was able to begin to recognize her own voracious needs.

This dynamic may also be expressed within an individual's imagery. One patient painted only abstract pictures of many colours merged together, with no form. She could make no sense of them but felt unable to do anything else. Her way of telling me about her lack of understanding gave me the feeling that I ought to be able (magically) to read her mind/be inside her and just know her, without this struggle for communication. I almost felt sucked in by her and by her images. This enabled me to appreciate what (on one level) she might want from/with me: a state of fusion where I could be inside her or she inside me, and therefore all-knowing.

This issue poses a potential problem for the art therapist. To try in some way to make sense of an image verbally must detract from the essence of the visual language. There cannot be an exact equation between image and words. It is important, therefore, how both therapist and patient make use of the images. If both collude in the belief that somehow the art therapist has a magic capacity to understand imagery fully, this falls directly into the patient's fantasy of symbiosis. The patient can then believe that she need not struggle to make sense of the image for herself because her other half, the therapist, will be doing the work for her.

The work in this case is thinking. It may hurt to think. The thoughts themselves may cause pain, for instance by bringing home an awareness of loss or of unmet wishes. Thus, the actual process of thinking for oneself, regardless of the content, may be resisted. To have one's own thoughts and to experience them as arising from within one's own mind implies that the same thing is happening within other people's minds. In other words, the patient and the therapist have different and therefore separate thoughts. This in turn forces an awareness of one's loss of magical control. No longer can the patient safely assume that the therapist will only be thinking the same thoughts as herself. This is the beginning of a sense of separate identity and carries with it great fear. It paves the way for a capacity for conflict and disagreement. It implies the need to tolerate not being fully understood and, most importantly, the capacity of both the self and the other to act independently. For these reasons I believe that it is an essential part of the art therapy process that patient and therapist face each other and express verbally their own thoughts arising from the image.

It must not be forgotten that for the patient with an eating disorder, who struggles so hard to demonstrate her self-sufficiency, the basic issues concern previously unmet dependency needs. A patient caught in any addictive cycle (be it related to food, drugs, alcohol or self-harm behaviours) has not learned to tolerate the experience of wanting and not being gratified. Her needs as a child were often perceived as greed, and therefore as excessive and destructive, and so may not have been adequately answered. The child, now in an adult's body, is still ranting and raving for her needs to be met; the adult equivalent of this is experienced as craving. It is much too dangerous for many patients to recognize just what it is that they are truly craving, because, once it becomes conscious, they become aware that they cannot fully control the supply that they need. The craving is transferred to something else. In anorexia, the reinforcing gratification comes from triumphing over the craving, which is held in contempt and viciously hated. A number of anorectic patients have painted images of voracious, screaming babies inside themselves, thereby conveying the sense in which this unacceptable part of themselves is split off and located in a separate object. The infant in the adult's body, who remains deprived, with needs unsatisfied, transforms the process of oral incorporation into the impulse to devour sadistically. It is this impulse that we see vividly portrayed in these images or in similar ones depicting devouring wild animals, or mouths biting at objects (see Figure 7.1).

The fundamental therapeutic aim in working with these patients is to facilitate the development of a secure, separate sense of self; to enable them to begin to recognize how many parts of themselves have become split off, disowned and denied because these have been considered so unacceptable both to themselves and, in fantasy, to others. Food abuse tries to disguise the panic arising from aloneness and separateness. The food addict desperately wants to create a substitute for a 'human drip' supplying comfort, one which she can turn on and off at will. The patient could thus have ultimate control of her food intake and the extent to which she relates to objects and other people. This also reflects the state of her inner world and the split off, fragmented parts within. Her symptoms can be understood to be an expression of this fragility and it is essential that the use of art therapy can be seen in terms of not only attempting to shore up the vulnerable self but also offering help in thinking about the relationship difficulties that result.

These relationship difficulties are expressed in the patient's

Figure 7.1

conflicting desires: to merge, and thereby deny separateness, followed immediately by a reaction against this; to accept the devouring need to have the other person inside herself, followed by denial and projection on to the other. She then becomes aware of her terror of the other person's demands or wishes to be close to her; the other's desire to engulf her or swallow her up. The patient is walking a tightrope between intimacy and closeness on the one hand and on the other the very negation of this, because of the potential destruction involved, which leads to the fear of aloneness, separateness and abandonment.

Some patients have come to recognize this pattern through exploring the process involved in creating their images. When their attention is drawn to the order in which the images are created, they find that they have continued to rework images of intense security, fusion and closeness, such as 'boxed in' images. They have made various changes, ranging from adding exits or openings to portraying explosions or total destruction. Within the art process this has occurred initially at a pre-verbal level, but it can then be expressed in words and introduced into the relationship between patient and therapist.

This fear of devouring is not confined to the actual images. Bulimic patients frequently describe 'bingeing on paint or paper' and often feel the need to binge on space, time and attention. Issues such as envy or fear of another patient over using some commodity can be utilized within the therapy. One patient expressed her fear that there would be nothing left if a certain bulimic patient did not restrain her use of vast quantities of materials. The former asked me fearfully how much money I had in the department budget and if I would be able to keep on providing the patients with materials. Indirectly she was expressing her fear of 'sucking me dry'. Her own desire to use up all of 'my' materials was evident in her frantic fear and her attempt to control anyone else's attempts to do so. Yet this patient was also terrified of her perceived capacity to devour and destroy me by her bingeing and by her enormous need. This need was not so much of me as a whole person but more as a source of a constant supply of something. Feelings of envy, jealousy and greed were being acted out in relation to each other, to the materials and to me. These feelings could first be dealt with on a concrete level with regard to the materials and then, when appropriate, be interpreted symbolically.

Co-existing with these feelings is the terror of needing, which underlies much of the tendency to resort to magic: no need will exist that cannot be met omnipotently by the person herself. There is a deep-rooted belief that to love or to possess the chosen object means to devour that person, which in turn necessitates destroying him/her. Guntrip (1982) describes this process as 'love made hungry', and suggests that this denial of need leads to the apparent aloofness often associated with anorexia. These patients feel the same about their empty stomach as they do about their empty feelings, just as the infant regards physical and psychological hurts to be the same.

This 'love made hungry' is directly linked to cannibalistic fantasies. There is a desperation to fill the empty space; a sense of hunger which may know no limits, which fuels the overwhelming desire to take in, possess, incorporate the wanted object. A striking image of this is offered by Pankow (1981) who describes the dream of a patient, Veronique, in which a man had cut off his own leg and put it in the refrigerator to eat, because he was nearly dying of hunger. Pankow describes this hunger as symbolic of the patient's inner emptiness which could be filled with the leg as food. Here the part of a former whole (leg of a body) has acquired a new existence as a whole in itself, with new meaing. The leg has become food. In interpersonal terms, this represents a part-object relationship (disguised as a whole-object relationship through the change in meaning).

This dream raises the question: to whom does the leg belong? Many patients with severe eating disorders have confused ideas about their own bodies and have difficulty in differentiating their body, or parts of it, from that of another person. Their boundary disturbance influences the effect of their incorporative fantasies, easily leading to experiences of fusion. Any reunion with an object is unconsciously thought of only in terms of eating the object. Magically the two will become the same substance.

Images of orality are repeatedly portrayed in patients' artwork: flies trapped in spiders' webs, vultures poised to eat their prey, cats pouncing on birds. 'To eat or be eaten' is the common theme associated with these images and describes the patient's fears in relation to all objects. The immediate identification is usually with the creature about to be eaten. In this way the patient's own hunger is denied and projected on to a cruel and sadistic other.

The images convey the horror of the patient's concept of relating. The two creatures cannot co-exist because one is overwhelmingly hungry and will therefore ignore the other's right to exist, that is, not be eaten.

One bulimic patient, who painted numerous images of herself pushing food into her mouth with the claws of a wild animal, demonstrated clearly the intensity with which she felt the need to binge (see Figure 7.2). When I told her that she had conveyed some of the anxiety in this picture to me, she replied, jokingly, 'I'm not surprised! You'd feel even worse if you knew what it [the animal] was eating.' Her fantasy appeared to be that she might wish to eat me up in such an animal manner. With this openly expressed, we were then able to explore issues within our relationship.

Figure 7.2

Another patient painted a picture of herself eating lots of choco-late bars on an underground train. When she was encouraged to associate freely with regard to the image, she connected bingeing on a tube train with being tube fed. The predominent experience of this was expressed by focusing on the tube-object as a part-object rather than on the feeding relationship between whole people which would involve an actual exchange and interaction in the use of a tube. She also associated being tube fed with being bottle-fed, and with oral sex. A number of other patients have also, through their imagery, associated their binges to some form of sexual contact. The sexual imagery of bulimics quite often includes powerful androgynous figures with which the patients associate the notions of needing no sexual partner and of being in control of all of their bodily needs.

These patients' imagery and use of art materials frequently reveal, in concrete and metaphorical ways, both their non-acceptance of needs (in particular those, such as feeding or sex, which are usually and most fully satisfied in an exchange relationship between whole people) and their attempts at keeping cannibalistic impulses under control. The next chapter will explore how these cannibalistic impulses exist and how they can be worked through within the therapeutic relationship.

Chapter 8

The therapeutic relationship

From the numerous concepts that have been developed in psychotherapy to illuminate the processes involved in both the therapeutic
relationship and the therapeutic setting, I should like to select
Winnicott's concept of 'potential space', which is particularly
valuable to the work of art therapists, especially with this patient
group. He describes potential space as a hypothetical area

> that exists (but cannot exist) between the baby and the object
> (mother or part of mother) during the phase of the repudiation of
> the object as not-me, that is, at the end of being merged in with
> the object.
>
> (Winnicott 1980)

The potential space in which play, creative acts or psychotherapy
occurs is, according to Winnicott, an intermediate area of experience. It lies between the inner world, that is, inner psychic reality,
and actual external reality. It lies between 'the subjective object and
the object objectively perceived, between me-extensions and not-
me' (1980). He describes how the potential space enables the
individual to communicate both directly and indirectly within it
and how it allows for the experience of being in touch with what
is 'other than me'. For separate individuals, mutuality is experienced and expressed in the overlap of potential spaces.

It is within this space that the individual can metaphorically be
held. The space is established and contained by the therapist for use
by both therapist and patient. It is the therapist's task to protect its
boundaries from any infringement by the outside world. This is of
particular importance for those who have not established their own
consistent boundaries and who have felt impinged upon by others.

The more borderline the eating-disordered patient's personality, the more diminished is her capacity to introject the 'external scaffolding' that is provided by a sense of being held.

The reason for these patients having such difficulty in this area can be directly linked to their resistance to taking in anything good and helpful, any nourishing food. As food is denied or vomited out, any useful external scaffolding, which is needed to lend support while the patient's internal structure strengthens, may unconsciously be torn down. It is important to become aware of when this happens. Although these patients have fragile boundaries, there is not necessarily constant boundary confusion (as in the case, perhaps, of an acutely psychotic patient). For a period of time these patients can maintain some sense of continuity in their identity and a degree of security within their body boundaries. Sometimes they can make use of external scaffolding, therefore it is helpful to work towards some understanding about points at which these fragile capacities break down. They may be broken down either consciously or unconsciously by the patient herself by the threat that is involved in maintaining stability. This threat should not be underestimated as there is an underlying gratification which arises from destabilization. The patient's hatred of having to do the work for herself (see Chapter 7, the resistance to thinking) can lead to a destructive attack on the good thing being offered, particularly when the aim of the proffered help is to enable the individual to do what is needed independently. This is not welcomed by the part of the patient that so desperately wants to recreate a dependent relationship in which she will be safely held.

Resisting any recognition of this state of affairs may mean that patients can make use of the art activities and the security of the art room only by denying that the art therapist plays any relevant part in the process. These patients may be able to continue with their work by making use of the art room between sessions with the therapist. This recreates the symbolic holding environment or the potential space. In this way the patients have some illusion of control. The room and the materials, which are associated with the experience of being safely held, are present at will.

I place great emphasis on the theme of being held. Many writers have described how these patients, who have an underlying borderline personality structure, experience problems in self-soothing. They have great difficulty in reducing uncomfortable states of tension by themselves. This is only one aspect of their experience and mainly affects the more severely disturbed end of the spectrum of eating disorders. The psychiatric diagnosis of Borderline Personality Disorder (BPD), which is based on a description of commonly found behaviours, is a much narrower concept than the psychoanalytic terminology which describes the way in which certain personalities are organized rather than behaviours. However, the common features described in BPD include impulsiveness, identity disturbance, intolerance of being alone, self-damaging acts, chronic feelings of emptiness – and the use of magical thinking: all familiar elements of eating disorders.

Goldstein (1985) emphasizes the problem that borderline patients have in holding and soothing and attributes their lack of capacity to a fault in the phases of separation–individuation. This, he suggests, leads to their dependency upon external objects to provide the necessary holding, which then maintains a sense of psychological integrity.

A moving description of what these patients may experience in not feeling securely held is given by Margaret Little:

> My fear was of utter destruction, being bodily dismembered, driven irretrievably insane, wiped out, abandoned and forgotten by the whole world as one who had never been – 'cast into outer darkness' (Matthew xxii, 13).
>
> (Little 1985)

She describes her analysis with Winnicott, who used the term 'holding' both metaphorically and literally. Little defines the former type of holding as 'taking full responsibility, supplying whatever ego strength a patient could not find in himself, and withdrawing it gradually as the patient could take over on his own' (1985). In other words, the therapist provided the facilitating environment in which the patient could feel safe.

Little describes the importance of the long periods of silence 'where nothing happened'. She could not talk until she felt sure that she would not be asked what she was thinking, that there would be no invasion of her space. 'It was as if I had to take into myself the silence and stillness that he [Winnicott] provided' (1985).

Although Margaret Little did not have an eating disorder, she experienced similar problems in relating. Anorectics frequently function in relation to 'part objects'. The other person, as a 'whole person', is excluded. Rycroft (1968) distinguishes a part object from a whole object by defining the former as:

> An object which is part of a person, e.g. a penis or a breast. The distinction . . . is sometimes used [to differentiate] between recognising an object as a person whose feelings and needs are as important as one's own and treating an object as existing solely to satisfy one's own needs.
>
> (Rycroft 1968)

Thus, what appears to be a relationship which is based on similar experiences may not be so. The symbolic exchange medium is different for both parties, since these patients have an impaired capacity to form symbols which may be traded within a relationship. This has important implications for the potential of art as a medium within the therapeutic relationship.

The therapist may find him/herself relating to a part of the patient. To communicate with the anorectic who has adopted a god-like posture with a sense of superhuman qualities and denial of the self, connection needs to be made with the part that is able to 'descend from heaven'. Of course, there is another side to this state: an unnamed nothingness which may be even more impossible to reach.

Fenichel (1946) describes some of these patients exhibiting

> Oral sadistic tendencies [which] are often vampire-like in character. Persons of this type request and demand a great deal, will not relinquish their object, and affix themselves by suction.
>
> (Fenichel 1946; see Figure 8.1)

Discussing the same stage, Guntrip (1982) explains that the infant (originally) regards any good object as an exciting breast to be captured by force and devoured. The infant may even depersonalize the object into a womb, a place in which to be safe. Achieving this in fantasy may result, however, in the smothering of the patient's own ego. It is as if he/she is in fear of being devoured. Guntrip relates the example of a patient who dreamed of fleeing from a monstrous mouth when in reality the person had fled from a good relationship.

In my experience many paintings by patients with eating disorders exemplify this theme. The extent to which such images may be understood in terms of a transference relationship, however, depends largely upon the capacity of the patient to engage in a whole relationship.

One bulimic patient painted violent, destructive pictures which often contained small images of hands and feet and, on one occasion,

Figure 8.1

lips chained together. She was unsure whether these parts of bodies belonged to her or to me. This woman appeared to feel 'whole' only when she had something of another person. For example, she frequently managed to win her father's attention away from her mother and this resulted in her feeling that, by owning/possessing her father, she became validated in some way. Of the hands and feet in her painting she said, 'I don't want them in my picture if they're yours.' While this seems to be a denial of how much she might actually want bits of me, it is more likely that she wanted these body parts, which she felt to be embodied in me, only in a transient way. Her wish for them not to be mine may have been to do with a need for me not to occupy her space within her painting. Her need was expressed in a variety of ways, such as requests for technical advice about the use of materials, or paintings apparently done for my approval.

These patients' difficulties in accepting their own needs seem closely linked to their cannibalistic fears. Simply expressing their needs within highly dependent relationships (such as those which many anorectics have with their families) does not fulfil these needs but merely perpetuates the addiction to a constant source of supply. It appears that the inability to bear their needy parts relates to the assumption that, if acknowledged, these would be so vast as to consume (and thereby destroy) the other. Similarly, to acknowledge the closeness, intimacy or need of another person would no doubt involve being consumed by his/her need. This may indeed be the experience of many anorectic patients in relation to their mothers, who, it has been noted, may narcissistically use their daughters to fulfil their own needs.

These ideas have implications for the way in which the art therapist works with these patients. For instance, the way in which the therapist conceives of these conditions will naturally influence his/her interventions. Bruch (1974) takes a firm view, which partially differs from my own, when she suggests that

> The more the disorder [anorexia] is conceived of as an expression of oral dependency, incorporative cannibalism, rejection of pregnancy, etc., the more likely one is to follow a classically psychoanalytic style of psychotherapy.
>
> (Bruch 1974)

Although this diverges from my line of thinking by rejecting the value of dealing with inter-psychic conflicts, I would agree with her views of abnormal eating as 'an effort to camouflage underlying problems, or build a defence against complete disintegration' (1974) and also her suggestion that therapy must aim at repairing the patient's underlying sense of incompetence, isolation and dissatisfaction. Even though this is a later development in the understanding of anorexia which places more importance on the failure of self-experience and on defective tools for organizing and expressing needs, I would suggest that the fear of disintegration is bound up with the cannibalistic impulses and fears that she partially rejects in her discussion.

These impulses and fears will be expressed by the patients in some form, whether through their imagery or their relationship with the therapist. The therapist in these cases is placed in a dilemma. In my experience there is often a powerful dynamic in the relationship whereby the patient expects to be 'fed' by the therapist but will often not digest the 'food'. For the therapist, the potential for becoming the supplier of 'food' is quite strong. However, the therapist who presumes to know all of the answers or to be a constant source of supplies (of understanding etc.) is actually serving the patient's magical belief that someone else knows everything that she thinks and will care for her *magically*. Bruch takes this idea further by emphasizing the importance of the therapist not working too inter-pretively. She suggests that it is very important to allow the patient to find her own meanings and not to increase her passive sense of mother always having known how she felt. If one accepts this practice, it has important implications for the way in which the art therapist should approach the patient's imagery or behaviour.

I would agree with Bruch that the use of interpretation should be carefully monitored, but not only for the reasons that she espouses. Another important reason is the tendency of these patients to operate in a concrete way, which makes it difficult for them to deal with symbolic interpretations and to enter into symbolic exchanges. The concept of concrete thinking will be explored more fully in Chapter 10 but it is worth mentioning here that Piaget related this to the stage of child development in which egocentricity is dominant. It involves preconceptual and concrete operations, where the capacity to perform abstract thought has not yet fully developed. Concrete thinking includes ideas such as that disciplining the body will magically result in personality change.

A further reason for curtailing the use of symbolic interpretations is that these can easily be experienced as invasive. Goodsitt (1985) states that, for patients with eating disorders,

> It is a well-integrated self that enables one to feel in control, and not just an empty receptacle easily distorted (fattened) or invaded by external forces – whether that external force is food or people.
>
> (Goodsitt 1985)

Thus, the link between feeling invaded and potentially devoured applies equally within the therapeutic relationship and every other sphere of these patients' lives. This has implications for the thera-pist's behaviour towards the patient. Goodsitt recommends that

> The therapist should allow the patient to do whatever [she] can reasonably accomplish without external assistance. The therapist will support the patient's independent functioning, but must be ready to step in and actively take over at a moment's notice.
>
> (Goodsitt 1985)

When the therapist intervenes actively he/she is, in a sense, acting as an 'external auxiliary ego' as part of the patient's own mental structure. This leads Goodsitt to conceptualize the role of the therapist as a 'transitional object'. No matter how the role is conceptualized, however, it is essential for the art therapist not to avoid but to respect the patient's fears concerning being engulfed.

One patient in a group painted a picture of sun, sea, a desert island and cannibals dancing around a pot (see Figure 8.2). A small boat was not far off the island. Her initial response to her picture was to describe it as inviting and pleasing. When asked to create a story from the picture she said that she was in the boat, approaching the island, and was full of good expectations until she saw the cannibals in the distance. She was then unsure about landing, since she did not know whether they would eat her or would be pleased at her arrival and suggest that she join in their dancing. It seemed as if she was expressing her uncertainty as to whether she was in danger of being consumed by (and into) the group (therapy group) or whether she actually identified with them (the cannibals). Was she to eat or be eaten? She decided that she was better off staying alone in her own boat, a position which she had in fact chosen for many years, having led a lonely, isolated life.

The way in which both therapist and patient make use of the art object is significant. Anorectic patients often feel that there is nothing to say about their work and they will proclaim, 'It doesn't mean anything.' Behind such a statement lies the inference, 'I'm not going to produce anything for you.' This is followed by, 'Well, what do you think it means, then?'; the implication being, 'I'm not going to work at this but I'd like you to do so.' In effect, the patient recreates a situation, possibly very familiar, in which the 'other person' did do something for (or instead of) her. If the therapist mishandles the situation, this can lead to him/her 'force-feeding' the anorectic with 'food' that she cannot possibly digest, because it is coming from an external source to which she is trying at all costs to refuse access.

The process of art therapy enables internal conflicts to be projected on to an external object (the paper) and allows for a form of visual feedback to reflect certain projected or disowned qualities. Although such feedback can be experienced also as threatening and intrusive, it is usually far less so than the feedback from the actual body of the therapist, who not only embodies the projections of the patient but also has the power of 'another' who has not been created by the patient.

Patients with eating disorders often refer to food as 'alien'. For them, it contains some magical power which, once incorporated, might do infinite damage inside. It therefore seems particularly

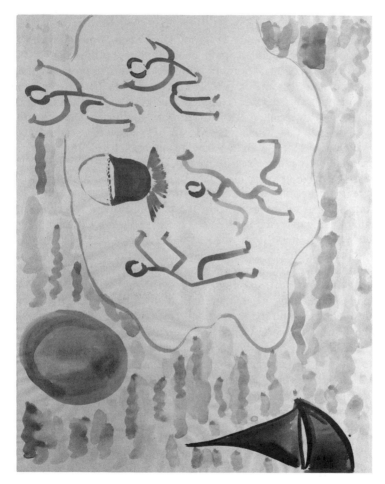

Figure 8.2

important that anything which is offered by the therapist should be 'digestible', with due respect paid to whatever the patient is able to take in from her own work, which is uncontaminated by anyone else.

This may be considered to be an important step in the development of the capacity to engage in a real relationship; a development which is not possible in the context of the patient's feeling that allowing another person to impinge upon her might have a devastating effect on her fragile sense of identity.

Whereas the patient may be employing various mechanisms in order not to feel impinged upon or devoured, the therapist in the counter-transference relationship may frequently feel precisely that. The therapist is often not perceived as a whole person, with an independent body; he/she is denied any personal feelings and is bombarded with demands to be 'fed with feelings'. The therapist may experience this as being taken over or swallowed up and it may be understood as the patient's desperate attempts, by identification, to incorporate the therapist's stronger ego. Guntrip (1982) suggests that the primary drive of every human is to become a person, to achieve a solid ego-formation, which can be done only in the medium of personal–object relationships. For the patient, however, any means will do to achieve this aim. Her need is for a constant external object which will keep her wholly and continuously gratified.

By obtaining this, the patient can fantasize that she is the source of the nourishment. When reality impinges, however, and proves to her that this is not so, she may react by (metaphorically) attacking the real source. It is clear, therefore, that these patients do create strong feelings in the therapist. I have found that a certain dynamic regularly occurs, whereby anorectic patients project their power into me, and so experience themselves as quite passive and helpless, while I feel an urge (greater than in relation to many other patients) to work hard 'for' them. Whenever I have succumbed to this state of affairs, the imbalance has unhelpfully increased and the patient has become more and more of a receptacle. As Boris (1984) points out:

> It is necessary to want nothing for or from the anorectic, though she will spare no effort to stimulate longing in the analyst. She will want to attend less frequently, say less, pay less – anything less. For her, of course, less is more . . . she will count on the analyst to demand *something* of her.
>
> (Boris 1984)

Boris explains that, in so far as the analyst begins to become an object of desire, the anorectic will begin to oscillate between finding the analyst's interest consuming and wanting to consume his/her interest. He suggests that this arises from the 'terrifyingly predatory intentions the anorectic has struggled to rid herself of, in an effort initally to save her mother from being cannibalised (1984).

Boris's understanding of the 'longings' that are created in the therapist relates to the anorectic's own longings which, having been denied so effectively, are projected on to the therapist. The anorectic then fears that she will be refilled with all that she has projected. R. D. Laing uses a concrete example of this process when he suggests that 'saliva, which is comfortable and familiar in one's mouth, once expectorated, even into a clear glass of pure water, is experienced as alien and repugnant' (Laing 1970).

To some extent, the anorectic patient has to face the reality of her situation with regard to feeling in tune with her activities and rituals. Whilst these may be seen as the symptoms of anorexia, until a profound change takes place they may be experienced by the patient as her salvation. If one accepts Bruch's definition of the therapeutic task as being to encourage an anorectic in her search for autonomy and self-directed identity in the setting of a new, intimate, interpersonal relationship, then the anorectic's way of dealing with her body and her relationships does indeed have to undergo a very significant change.

The issue of space and territory is of great importance to patients with eating disorders because of their cannibalistic fears and longings and it must be addressed. In this case, 'space' refers to both the emotional space between therapist and patient and the actual space in relation to the patient's artwork. In both the relationship and the artwork may be seen the constant conflict for these patients between the desperate longing for closeness or merger and the terror of being engulfed if they were to give in to their desire. The need to achieve the desired and to prevent the feared is very powerful and is accompanied by strong body sensations and by feelings. Thus, patients with eating disorders use potent means to control their space, including the degree to which they 'allow in' the therapist. He/she may be kept out by the patients' lack of verbal responses, by the mass-production of images or by the refusal to consider any interpretations. The importance lies in recognizing the underlying fear of letting 'in' somebody or something, that is, of being cannibalized. Patients will express that fear, sometimes directly, more often indirectly, in the form of controlling behaviour. Usually is not difficult for them to recognize and accept their need to be in control, but they find it far less easy to recognize and accept what it is that they need to control. The degree to which they feel threatened by the potential invasion of the therapist may commonly be seen in their attempts to prevent the therapist from empathizing with them. Even this is felt to be an intrusion, a taking over.

One patient, in art therapy sessions with me, had refused for a long time to paint or draw. In my attempt to understand, with her, the meaning of this, I became aware of my feelings in relation to her. I felt pushed away and rejected by this patient who did not want what I was offering. Eventually what became more apparent than the meaning of this act (which could have been acted out in any other way) was the effect that it had: she created a greater space between us while I tried to reduce the distance. This helped me to understand her perception of my intrusiveness, as she had picked up that I expected something from her.

As a result of this understanding I changed the way in which I related to her and she, in turn, felt safe enough to use the session more 'productively'. Another aspect of her behaviour, her denigration of me, served to prevent her from wanting anything good from me. Boris's view (as previously described) of the need for the therapist to want nothing was again highly relevant. This patient was defending herself (most effectively) against her fierce longings. If I had 'taken them in' and had 'acted out her longings', she would have intensified her distancing even further. She expected me to understand her either magically or telepathically. However, since this process could easily have become persecutory, I was just to 'hold' her, with full knowledge of her, as if we were one.

With relation to space, it is equally important for the therapist to take into account what is *not* painted, by looking at the space left between images or used instead of images. The anorectic who does not paint a whole body (see Figure 8.3) or the bulimic who cannot permit herself to leave any space at all on the paper are two examples of cases where space becomes significant. For some patients, being faced with a large sheet of blank paper may reflect their fear of the empty spaces inside that they often describe as frantically having to fill up with food.

If the art therapist uses the patient's artwork as a means of exploring the relationship between them, many images become significant. Through understanding that the desire for/fear of intrusion and devouring reigns supreme, a common feature of anorectic art becomes apparent, namely the frequency with which the anor-

Figure 8.3

ectic portrays herself in some concrete and significant way as different from her family or others. She may be a different shape, symbol or colour or else separated by a boundary of some sort (see Figure 8.4). Images of self-protection, of separateness or of non-belonging constitute the anorectic's means of *survival*. By being 'different' and separate from the group, she is seeking to establish some identity 'of her own' which cannot be merged with that of the others. To be the same colour, size or symbol as 'the other' implies being swallowed up (and annihilated) by that person's more domi-nant identity. Many anorectics are unable to conceive of their

Figure 8.4

having a human body at all (as demonstrated by the meagre pin figures or lack of body definition in their artwork).

The reduced capacity of patients with eating disorders to allow ambivalent feelings is also frequently represented in their artwork. Their radical 'single-mindedness' shows itself in the use of materials, in the 'colouring' of the theme and in the 'black-and-white evaluation' of their work (that is, the work is either wholly good or bad). It is important for the therapist to display the capacity to tolerate his/her own ambivalent feelings. By doing so, the therapist is facilitating the potential space, the setting for a relationship which need not be either all-consuming or totally abandoning.

In one session, an anorectic painted a strange, circular, worm-like creature, with no particular beginning or end. She associated this image with an animal who fed itself, from within its own body, and so was quite self-sufficient. Certainly this creature had similar features to those of the mythological Uroboris, a snake or dragon that eats its own tail. It is a symbol both for individuation as a self-contained circular process and for narcissistic self-absorption. I understood this image to relate to the patient's fear of allowing herself to experience any needs in her relationship with me. Her demeanour was aloof and controlled. She had created a self-contained vacuum. I could not distinguish any part of her; had I been able to, perhaps she might have felt that I would then have had greater access to her. As it was, she identified with the creature in feeling that she was something quite different from me, and so I was firmly excluded.

The body of the patient with an eating disorder becomes the battleground over which she fights not only with her internalized parental figures but also with her own instincts, drives and human qualities which prevent her from becoming a powerful 'spirit' god. The enlarging or the decreasing, the punishing and the destroying of her own body are the overt signs of the battle, which is truly one for the survival of mind/spirit/ego at the cost and peril of the body.

The anorectic is fighting her body because she considers it to be, first, the concrete manifestation of the unacceptable part of herself (passive receptiveness) and, second, the territory or base of an all-powerful, alien invader (feelings indicate its presence). The battle is likely to be re-enacted within the therapeutic relationship because the patient has developed a survival 'tactic', which depends upon her not giving in (or giving up control). To accept from another person anything which threatens this posture is to lose the battle for her own sense of self.

It is essential that such conflicts are brought out in the therapeutic relationship so that they may be worked through. In residential institutions, the regular battles for control, if handled sensitively, can provide the basis for work to begin on the twin issues of who controls whose body and whether whole-person relationships are annihilating or life-enhancing.

'I've just got to hold myself together,' said one patient after painting a pin figure whose arms were copiously wrapped around its match-like body. If she were to risk involvement, by allowing another to help to hold her together, she might be let down. Because the anorectic (in particular) sets such standards of perfection for herself and the world, no one is likely to be good enough or able enough to reach them. Associated with this is the fantasy or belief that, if she were to push herself hard enough, she would be capable of superhuman feats, in contrast to mere mortals who are doomed to constant failure and are at the mercy of their bodily functions.

Thus, the therapist is perceived as a combination of an idealized source of magical supplies, which dare not be desired, and an object to be despised or denigrated. Since the development of a whole-person relationship is a fundamental aim of the therapeutic work, which is frequently and powerfully defeated by the patient (leading to potentially life-endangering situations for her), an intermediate area of relating must be created in order to facilitate development (and save life).

I suggest that the involvement of the patient in the creation of artwork, using concrete, durable imagery, in the presence of a facilitating therapist may be regarded as an important step towards the development of a whole-person relationship. The 'taking in' something from a self-made object/image is not experienced as a devastating intrusion which threatens the patient's already fragile sense of self. Yet, the image is created and spoken about in a setting which includes the (whole person) therapist. A link is established and an intermediate area for therapeutic work is created. Boris (1984) describes how

> the anorectic does not wish to want, she wishes to be the object of the others' wants. What earlier she achieved by docile co-operativeness, later she will achieve by stimulating people to want her to eat. Therefore yearning is transferred to abstinence, and retention to elimination. Anorectics cannot bear to receive because they want to possess. They wish to stimulate desire and envy in the other – and therefore become the object, not the subject.
>
> (Boris 1984)

Since the therapist has difficulty with working directly with the patient, Boris suggests that the therapist should work in a transitional space, should talk to the air as if confiding in an interested but occupied colleague. The air, as the transitional space, confirms the anorectic's boundaries, so that, to use Boris's concept, there will be less need for the 'in-me space but not of-me space' (1984).

Sprince (1984) also discusses the concept of the use of space. She suggests that the 'anorectic avoids the pain of emptiness by denying the empty space and concretely decreasing the void. The bulimic seeks endlessly to fill the space' (Sprince 1984). She maintains that these patients use their analyst as if he/she were the 'missing part' of themselves, the part that they can no longer replace by food. She suggests that this stage is crucial in the treatment, because the defences against engulfment or devastating separateness are threatened in the transference.

Chapter 9

Why art?

The use of art in the therapeutic process is a viable alternative to verbal language, in that it may bypass the verbal defences of patients with eating disorders, many of whom are well educated and articulate, and may instead encourage a more appropriate form of communication for that pre-verbal area to which many of their problems belong.

Many writers, such as Meyer and Weinroth (1957), have expressed doubts as to the effectiveness of verbal forms of treatment for a condition which has its origins in the pre-verbal period of development. Pickford (1967) suggests that, through art, one can help the patient 'to realize his unconscious fantasies symbolically and to bring them into the scope and control of his ego'. Art may also allow the patient to express that which she lacks the words to describe. A patient with an eating disorder (in common with those suffering from some psychosomatic conditions) does not express her conflicts through the use of psychological, symbolic metaphors. To encourage her to create and to relate to a concrete object may therefore provide an intermediate step towards the development of symbolizing functions and symbolic exchange relationships. Through the use of art, the intensive psychotherapeutic relationship is deflected from the direct immediacy of two people.

In relationships, the patient with an eating disorder experiences herself as acting only in response to the demands of others. Her body does not belong to her. When she 'gives in', she feels powerless, ineffective and lacking in core personality. 'Giving in' may include almost any act of acceptance. The act of painting, however, may help to lessen the defiant defensive mechanism that she so frequently uses. By expressing something of her own, on paper, it becomes clear to her that whatever she creates belongs to her; it has not been pushed into her or on to her paper, and she has some substance in relation to it.

An anorectic, who described a sense of having no self, painted over an outline of her body shape which had been pencilled in around her. She tried to fill in the shape but felt quite unable to do so. Instead she frantically obliterated the body boundary by scribbling over the whole sheet. In effect, she obliterated herself. The realization that she actually occupied a certain amount of space in the world was intolerable to her. This presented her with the experience of two incongruities – visual evidence of her bodily existence drawn on paper and her own perception of not existing.

A bulimic patient responded differently to the same technique. She spent most of the session going over and over her outline (i.e. the body boundary) with thick black paint, to the exclusion of painting anything inside the body. For her, it was essential that she 'didn't go over the edge', because she feared that her body contents might spill out on to the rest of the paper if not securely contained within this barrier. Alternatively, the outside world might penetrate inwards. Her desperate need for containment and for external boundaries was thus highlighted by the activity. This enabled us to explore the extent to which the thickening of the boundary served to protect her, by delineating the separateness between her and me.

Another patient, a very disturbed borderline woman with an extreme degree of bulimia, noticed that all of the shapes that she painted were of bodies. It was as if she could use only her body to express herself, either literally or pictorally. Some crucial questions for her were: how much space do I take up in relation to others? What happens at the interface of two bodies meeting? Do they merge to become one and thereby lose their separate selves? Is it possible to retain a self when in relation to another? Where do I exist: inside my whole body or just in parts of it? Is a body constant and is it as reliable as a self?

These themes emerged from her use of imagery. She always painted a distinct coloured background which caused her odd formless shapes to stand out. Similarly, she wore very striking, seductive and (for midwinter) scanty clothing, causing her to stand out too. Her fear was of not being seen. If she were not seen, perhaps she did not really exist. If she did not have physical contact with others, she might disappear. Hence, between her periods of bulimia, she prostituted herself, with little interest in the financial gains.

Indeed, her need for contact was so great and her lack of boundaries so pronounced that she also engaged in sexual activities with all of her young children.

One of her paintings was of two 'blobs' set against a startling, bright turquoise background. She worked hard at emphasizing the black boundary around each of the two forms. She used a very wet brush and so splashed some water on to her paper. This caused one black line to run and to melt into the other blob. She reacted strongly to this 'accident'. Whilst painting, she explained, all that she had been aware of was the need to prevent these forms from touching. Seeing them join brought to mind her terror at her inability to set limits and boundaries, particularly with regard to her small daughter. She was scared to smack her, in case she proceeded to kill her; to kiss her, since this would lead to more sexual contact; to play with her physically, as she watched other mothers do with their children, in case she ate her. She talked of the way in which 'normal mothers' would play with their children and say such things as, 'I could eat you all up'. She referred to games in which mothers would pretend to be about to eat their children's fingers or toes. For her, the threat of intimate contact was clear; her desire to incorporate the outside world, to have everything inside her, so that there was no such thing as outside and inside or separateness, was so great that she felt that she was a danger to others.

Her need for each of the forms to be confined within its own black boundary related not only to containing separate body substances but also to delineating where the bodies actually were in relation to each other. She created images of herself which, like an etching, had texture and contrast, because without these (in the extreme) she feared that she would have no tangible substance. For her, bingeing and vomiting made her feel real, feel full, and thereby feel a body. The process of pushing things in and out of her own body could create a delineation between inside and outside the body. The magical action could create a self for her. The in–out differentiation, which was observed physically in her bulimic behaviour and visually in her art (in terms of the spatial use of foreground and background dimensions), was more apparent to her than the other relationships, such as that existing between parts of her body and the whole.

Another bulimic patient, who did not want to appear greedy (in my eyes) by using extra sheets of paper, painted on both sides of a sheet. On one side, she painted a very large fish about to swallow up lots of tiny fish. On the other side there was a fragmented and chaotic picture which was frightening as it was made up of dismembered parts of human bodies. She said that she would rather be a fish than a human, as long as she was a big fish which could not be eaten like a little fish. Her means of organizing and containing the scattered pieces of bodies in the other picture was apparently linked to her fantasy of being the big fish and swallowing up everything around. If she could have all those pieces inside her, she would have 'beaten the elements'. The theme of competition suggested that she might wish to beat not only the elements but also another person (her mother or me) in competition for the phallic-looking arms and legs. This patient had a very clinging and dependent relationship with her mother, which suggested the presence of a defensive function in her artwork, namely a retreat from competing with her mother.

This patient needed (and achieved through her bulimia) a constant means of rekindling her internal representation of a nurturing mother figure. I was not allowed to escape this projection. She repeatedly resorted to using her own body to recreate the issues of taking in and getting rid of the other person. This was evident both in her imagery and in the therapeutic relationship. She was able to move from using her own body to using 'a body of art' as a transitional object, which permits more experimentation but with less danger. Transformations in the 'body of art' can be observed and influenced from outside the body where change occurs. Art can provide a means by which such a patient may begin to define herself, other than through her own body. By creating external objects, the patient may also be her own creator.

Guntrip (1982) describes anorexia as 'hardly so much a symptom, as a guiding principle of life'. The removal of the symptom is therefore resisted with tremendous force. The anorectic will typically perceive all attempts at change as being forced upon her, so that a power battle ensues. Using art as a medium through which the patient can face essential issues, outside the struggle for control, means that the battle is no longer directly between two human bodies but via an intermediary (non-human) body which has been made by the patient and not by the therapist.

A bulimic patient created a self-figure out of clay which she called 'the Statue of Liberty'. She spent a disproportionate amount of time on making its base. She talked about the need for some resistance in the material with which she chose to work; it required enough 'body' to be able to resist her push. Her feelings of omnipotence, of being able to control her mother at will, left her with not only a frightening sense of power but also a fear that no one could possibly contain or restrict her. Her concentration on the base of this statue led to her acknowledging her need to create literally a firm base for herself.

Art may be seen as an extension of the self and as a psychological double capable of mirroring oneself. Kohut describes the anorectic as someone who lacks the consistent mirroring that leads to the development of the self. Art may also be used to examine violent feelings. The magical omnipotence of a bulimic patient was tested in this way, through her violent, destructive paintings. She felt sure that her family could not possibly withstand her destructive feelings, and so she had to 'swallow' the ones she loved in order to protect them.

Pickford (1967) states that 'Art is . . . in part a process of ego defence, by which fantasies are . . . exteriorized by projection, and in part a therapeutic process, by which the ego may find out that its most dangerous fantasies are harmless.' This is true even when the patient acts out her aggression on the 'body of art', using harsh brush strokes or scratching through thick layers of paint (commonly found in the artwork of bulimics). Pickford suggests that these acts may represent an unconscious substitution for a more meaningful person or object. Pencil scoring may even represent an oral attack, as a substitute for the teeth.

Psychoanalytic ideas inform us that sexual and aggressive impulses, when characterized by an overwhelming compulsive quality, are a response to frustration or deprivation, which may exist in the external and/or internal world. An impulsive drive is associated with a tendency to action. Severe repression causes primitive impulses to be denied until they reach a state of explosive tension. When they break through, actions, such as criminal damage or (in this field); binges, may occur. In the art therapy setting, understanding the potential cannibalistic aspects of a binge aids recognition of the above-mentioned emotions and dynamic patterns.

Such behaviour is often observed during art therapy. Some anorectics will eventually react against their tight, controlled pencil drawings on small sheets of paper and will give way to a chaotic 'binge' on materials, although this occurs more frequently amongst the bulimic patients. This form of 'acting out' is associated with the patient's recognizing that to do something provides some sort of relief (as would bingeing or vomiting). Primarily, however, the capacity to think is overtaken by the need to act, in response to the internal build-up of tension. Since control over the impulse to act is weak and since the relief obtained is temporary, there are grounds for 'having to' act again.

Many patients with eating disorders describe the process of painting as feeling like a binge. Indeed large quantities of paper and art materials are sometimes 'consumed'. There are certain similarities. There is a temporary loss of boundaries, during which the patient merges with the object. There is accompanying heightened stimulation and relief at being able to carry out the action. It is important, therefore, to distinguish between encouraging a form of behaviour (acting out) which could perpetuate defensive modes of dealing with conflict and utilizing an activity which, whilst used in a similar way, offers therapeutic potential.

Unlike the secretive binges on food, these 'alternative' binges within the therapeutic setting do not result in the patient feeling distraught, guilty and full of self-reproach. Thus, feelings which were present just prior to the impulsive use of materials are more easily accessible. The therapist can therefore be involved in a non-punitive way and there is an opportunity to recognize the motivations behind the 'binge', almost as it is happening.

This exploration of motives may not be purely verbal. It may involve the therapist in being aware of the way in which the patient works on her painting, the progression of image creation – the style and content – or of image destruction. The action is a means of expressing physically what cannot easily be tolerated in feelings, thoughts or words.

Whilst the patient is involved in the activity, the therapist must retain the capacity to think. However, after the painting has been completed, the therapist must ensure that he/she is not unconsciously made to take over the patient's capacity to think. For staff working with patients who 'act out' their feelings to a large extent, it is quite common to feel that they are being forced into behaving in a certain way or into taking some action; in other words, they are acting out something for the patient. This manifests itself in the art therapist's strong desire to make associations or interpretations which are acutely connected to the images produced. Through the activity, the patient has meanwhile emptied her mental contents on to the paper and now feels quite blank, which seems to be a function of the symptom. Such a patient is unable to tolerate or hold on to discomfort. It needs to be magically controlled or eliminated in some way. In relation to another person, the patient's wish may be for that other person to 'hold' or contain these uncomfortable parts for her. It is quite appropriate for the therapist to go along with that wish temporarily, provided that he/she can judge the stage at which the patient is ready to reclaim the projected parts, thereby diminishing the potential experience of her being swallowed up by the other person.

The therapist should therefore be helping the patient to find ways in which the activity can serve as a means of communication rather than emptying out. The fact that these patients operate mostly on a concrete level has important implications for the use of art therapy. Pankow (1961) suggests that, because psychotic or borderline psychotic patients live largely in a world of concrete objects, therapeutic work must first be directed at increasing their capacity to symbolize, before they are able to engage in a relationship. She discusses the use of art or making objects in therapy as these are concrete. 'These objects allow for an expression of the individual's own body experiences, into an object which can be manipulated, allowing in a sense, a playground for rudimentary object relations' (Pankow 1961).

Some parallels may be drawn here with Klein's use of toys, although Klein employed this approach in therapy with children and she believed that even very small infants, as well as psychotic adults, function and relate symbolically. Pankow, however, maintains that psychotic patients have no capacity to relate symbolically to part or whole objects because they are fragmented, they have lost the form (container) for the self and so have lost the symbolizing functions of the body image. Pankow uses art objects as intermediaries in an attempt to create a structure for the self, a body image, which is as a necessary precondition for the ability to enter into symbolic exchange relationships.

Once art objects have been created within the therapeutic setting, patients can be encouraged to give the concrete image a self-created context of relationships 'outside' of themselves and of the therapist by creating a fantasy story in which all or part of the concrete image participates. The emphasis is thereby removed from the 'self' and placed on to/into the world of concrete object relationships, which is built from fragments of self, and which involves the therapist in communicating through both the objects and the fantasies of the fragmented patient. Pankow's initial focus is upon the recognition and structure of spatial order, and the establishment of outline and form. It is clear, therefore, how important these ideas are not only to the understanding of the development of body boundaries but also to the potential use of images and art objects in the process of altering the dynamics of self and other both for psychotic patients and for borderline psychotics who only intermittently or partially function on a psychotic level.

A concrete level of functioning implies that thought and meaning are literal rather than metaphorical. It involves a greater degree of the primary process style of thought. Paintings or clay models have tangible boundaries which can be worked with more safely by patients whose own boundaries are so nebulous. Words may be potentially dangerous because they can invade the other's space. Artwork has a concrete means of expression which words lack. A feeling can be literally seen or touched.

Paintings may evoke awareness in the patient of impulses, feelings or needs which originate within her and so are not put there by somebody else. The painting 'speaks out of its own body'. It acts as an intermediary body between patient and therapist and so may prevent the therapist from working directly on the patient's body.

Selvini Palazzoli (1974) suggests that

> It is thanks to the analysis of concrete events and actions that the therapist can help the patient open himself to abstract thought – a difficult but indispensable journey if the patient, is to resolve the apparent contradiction between his . . . body, . . . and the body as a meaningful structure.
>
> (Palazzoli 1974)

This concrete level of thinking is described, within the definition of 'symbolism' given by Laplanche et al. (1983), as that 'in which unity exists between the satisfying object (e.g. the breast) and its symbol (e.g. apples)'.

An art therapist working with these patients must understand the nature of the concrete metaphors that they use, in relation to both their imagery and their means of dealing with their own body and that of others. Initially a patient may not be able to relate to the therapist as a whole person. Instead, the therapist is merely a body which the patient can act upon (i.e. do things to or take things from). This perception of the therapist remains until it becomes integrated with that of having a permanent body, to which the patient can relate and which can be internalized.

A patient may be able to use body-centred experiences more successfully than symbolic work, particularly in the early stages of therapy. Thus, interpretation of the content produced is only one part of the therapeutic work. During one session, a patient appeared quite unconsciously to imitate many of my movements and mannerisms as we discussed her painting. I even heard my own voice inflection coming from her. She was particularly interested in a technique in which a shape is painted thickly on one side of a sheet of paper, which is then folded to produce a mirror image. After the session I realized that, rather than focusing upon her associations to the shapes that she had produced (Rorschach style), it would have been more appropriate to have explored the relationship between that particular technique and her mirroring of me. Both seemed to produce a combined reflection, a state of connectedness. It appeared that her fusion with me had been displayed concretely through both the choice of art technique and her adoption of my mannerisms. She even displayed an avid interest in creating replicas of the produced images.

This session highlighted another aspect of the issue of space, namely body presence and the form of relating. At a distance, the patient was aware of the whole of me. When close by, however, she became aware only of my hands which were involved in demonstrating an image-making activity. I, as a person, almost disappeared. For such patients, 'parts' merely exist; they come from nowhere and lead nowhere. They are *unrelated*. This remains the case until the individual comes to relate parts to a whole object, which exists in time and space. To relate to an object, in terms of its potential for 'supplies', is to relate to only a part of it. The satisfaction is then directed to the possession of such parts (see Figure 9.1).

This lack of symbolic capacity is also demonstrated by these patients' experience of their own bodies. Being fat is perceived as a public display of lack of control, of greed; it is a concrete symbol of everything bad inside. The anorectic will firmly believe that the cause of her despair is the fact that her body shape is too fat, and so she will attempt to deal with the feelings by concrete manipulation of her body.

In relation to symbolic capacity in the use of art, it would be wrong to equate symbolic functioning only with a healthy mental state. Rycroft (1968) defines symbolism as 'the capacity of mind which may be used by the primary or secondary process,

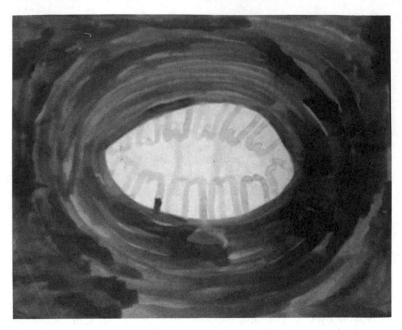

Figure 9.1

neurotically or realistically, for defence or self-expression to maintain fixation or to promote growth.' However, according to Brown
(1985), when a patient is largely restricted to the use of concrete
functioning, this causes the 'patient's imprisonment in a current
situation . . . that casts a shadow of narrow meaning across all
experience' (Brown 1985).

Brown divides concrete thinking into three categories: topographical, semiotic and interactional, all of which have relevance
to working with these patients. Topographical concrete thinking
refers to the substitution, in place of a higher mode, of a lower
mode of experiencing an event, such as occurs in 'acting out' when
action replaces verbal expression. Patients with eating disorders act
out their feelings in the realm of their own bodies, and so they are
restricted to the use of a bodily language.

Semiotic concreteness occurs when there is a confusion between a
sign and that which it signifies. A word may be taken to be the
equivalent of that to which it refers; a visual image may occur in
place of a thought. Such confusion results from the obliteration of

boundaries and is therefore highly relevant to interpersonal relationships.

Interactional concrete thinking occurs when a patient is confused by the use of words which seem impenetrable or dense. The patient, although bright, cannot understand the therapist's intentions. Brown defines this as a form of resistance which stems from the inability to take in interpretations.

The difficulty in taking in anything from another, which is experienced by patients with eating disorders, was described earlier as involving fears of invasion and engulfment. Art materials exist outside of the patient. Through creative work, however, internal aspects are projected outwards on to the paper and may be taken back inside at will. There is therefore some room for psychological manoeuvre amongst individuals who are wholly preoccupied with what may go into their bodies and what may be taken out.

Art materials not only permit an exploration of the concrete issues concerning the body but also, because of their 'messiness' and tactile quality, promote associations about bodily substances. The expressionist art of Oskar Kokoschka was described by art critic Peter Conrad (1986) as being 'about the pressing out of morbid secretions from within – Kokoschka identified paint with the gushing of blood or the suppuration of wounds'. Marion Milner, an artist and psychoanalyst, in discussing art imagery comments on the 'innate tendency to apprehend all objects that are *not* one's self, by likening them to bodily organs and processes – enabling us to assimilate the outside world to the primordially familiar world of our own bodies' (Milner 1952).

Many patients want to make 'a mess' with the paints, either as a reaction to orderliness or as an external expression of what they feel that they contain inside them (see Figure 9.2). Schilder (1970) describes how there is also a desire to gain knowledge by touch, a curiosity concerning the surface of the body, the skin, and also its inner contents. He states: 'When we have satisfied the eye, we use tactile experience and we want to intrude into every hole of our body with our fingers' (Schilder 1970). Smearing is considered by some analysts to involve a primitive manifestation of anal eroticism. Although I have focused upon the incorporative aspects of eating disorders, the elimination and expulsion of inner body contents is, of course, the other important dimension. These aspects are also related to ways in which the patient attempts to control her body magically. Fenichel (1946) describes how the pleasure of elimination

Figure 9.2

is first experienced at a time when the 'Primary feelings of omnipotence are still operative [and] can be seen in magical narcissistic overvaluation of the power of the individual's bowel movement' (Fenichel 1946).

Very often patients with eating disorders are rigid and extremely uncomfortable with their own bodies, which they wear like a pair of ill-fitting shoes. The process of painting, whether it is done with an obsession to get it right, to compress space or to expand over a large area of paper, allows the individual to move around within a contained space, in a manner which promotes awareness of the body. During the activity, the use of materials can be met with some resistance. The patient is dealing with a concrete external object which has a defined space. This sets up a contrast to her own disembodied experience and can provide bodily feedback through the recognition of feelings and sensations. Through the desire to splash paint, to press harder with crayons or to cut and tear, impulses originating within the body, which have been both emotionally and physically denied, are experienced and communicated.

In this way the imagery can be used as a kind of reflector which also increases bodily awareness. Blank and empty spaces, for example, are associated with those same feelings. An anorectic patient in one art therapy session painted a self-portrait in white paint on white paper, literally making herself invisible. She commented that there was an issue of her not being 'seen or heard' within her family. On another occasion, she responded to a white patch, which she had already painted on the white paper, by covering it up with black paint. In quick succession, she painted over this with white, then black, and so on. In discussion, she said that the white had frightened her and that she had wanted to cover it up. Then the black had concerned her because she felt that she was covering up something. She associated this with feeling invisible in her family; with how they appeared to 'look right through her' as if she did not exist, 'just like the white paint on the paper'. She said that she was scared of admitting to some of her feelings and that she did not want her family (or me) to 'see through her entirely'. She began to connect the process of obscuring white with black with her desire to obscure parts of herself in my eyes, so that I too would not be able to see her properly.

The making of art also affords an opportunity for reparation. Kleinian theory would suggest that the process of giving symbolic expression in art to the libidinal and destructive forces of the unconscious is accompanied by compensatory fantasies of reparation. With reference to oral cannibalistic fantasies of attacks on the mother, the use of art allows for the 'making whole again' of the 'broken object'. This has been demonstrated on a number of occasions by patients who, wishing to 'repair', paint over certain images or patch together torn-up pieces of paper. The feelings that they associated with the destructive acts were also related to tearing things apart like wild animals. Destroying and repairing an inanimate (art) object not only expresses otherwise unconscious (animate) fantasies and makes them available for conscious recognition and reflection but also creates a new concrete reality experience, which can be internalized and which can thereafter alter the nature of internal object relations.

The magical omnipotence of destructiveness and of reparation is first acted out (in art therapy) with a concrete object standing in for the unconscious, symbolic, internal object. This process then facilitates a resymbolization through the perception of the concrete act in a different setting; that is, 'acting out' is now used as a magical reorganization of reality.

The basic association between art and magic is again underlined. Observations by psychoanalysts about art and magic in general can be utilized productively in art therapy. Freud describes how the function of art was originally to work in the service of impulses, which included many magical purposes. Primitive artists produced carvings and paintings of animals in order to evoke spirits. Modell (1969) reflects psychoanalytically on Palaeolithic cave paintings:

> In the cave paintings life is both created and destroyed. Cave art functions as a creative illusion, an illusion that provides for the participant a sense, through symbolic representation, of mastery, a mastery of the elemental forces of life and death. Action upon the symbolic animal influenced the 'real' animal, creating a world that acknowledged no distinction between symbol and object, a world that was created in accordance with omnipotent wishes . . . . The paintings of the Palaeolithic period can be interpreted as symbols of objects that they denote, but there is little doubt that for Cro-Magnon man they were not symbols: the paintings and statues were the animals, and action upon the image would affect the object. The wishes expressed by means of magical thinking are determined by 'real' needs and are the direct response to 'real' dangers of the environment. There is a striking parallel between the response to a situation of helplessness, or, as we shall now say, anxiety, of Palaeolithic man and the response to a situation of helplessness in the modern infant and child.
>
> (Modell 1969)

There is a striking parallel here with the problems of patients with eating disorders. The dangers which are perceived by them to be 'real' in their concrete environment (including their body) can gradually be 'mastered' via the concrete body image-making which, in the setting of art therapy, facilitates symbolization beyond the repetition of 'primitive' magical thinking and acting.

Art therapy allows the patient to move into an intermediate area of experience which is situated between her internal and external realities and yet which is contained and bounded not only by the edge of the materials but also by the holding space of the therapeutic environment and relationship.

Chapter 10

Conclusion

What actually happens during the therapeutic process which enables many patients with eating disorders to take the necessary risks involved in progressive change? The course of events may be understood through the patient's artwork and her developing relationship with her images. In the early stages of treatment, images are spilled out on to the paper; much of this work has little or no form. Emotions are literally poured out in paint, sometimes over the edges of the paper on to the table, and images are not contained within separate forms.

Any creative work involves a degree of controlled regression, but this is seldom exhibited by these patients. Instead, as Kramer reports,

> we are used to seeing paintings of volcanoes become a mass of red and black because explosive feelings were not depicted but acted out. We see carvings end up as pieces of wood because the acts of cutting unchains aggressive drives that cannot be confined within a given shape.
>
> (Kramer 1975, quoted in Case and Dalley 1992)

It is crucial for the patients that the art therapist distinguishes between therapeutic enactment of certain feelings and anti-therapeutic forms of acting out. In the early stages, the patient often merely wishes to rid herself of uncomfortable feelings and art is seen as another means by which she can do this. The process itself can be highly charged and may invite regressive behaviours. At such times the patient's own observing ego, that part of herself which can stand back from the activity and recognize what she is doing, is not present. There is a need for some capacity to remain distanced and separate from her own behaviour, in order to be able to have thoughts about it. This may be relinquished because it would keep a tight rein on her behaviour, which is far less immediately gratifying to a patient who is longing to empty herself. During these stages it is the art therapist who at first carries this observing part of the patient and who feeds back to her what he/she perceives as happening.

Thus, at first, the patient replaces her thinking processes with behaviour, and that form of 'acting out' may well be brought into the art therapy session. Any subsequent change depends upon the relationship between the patient and therapist, through which the patient develops a growing awareness of the context in which her behaviour is occurring. The therapist indicates the limits that are acceptable for the behaviour and so the patient's original impulses have to be sufficiently modified or symbolically translated into an acceptable means of expression. The therapist may intervene during this process to make suggestions or to help the patient to become aware of the symbolic nature of the activity, in effect to regain her thinking capacity about herself. As Kramer (1977) describes, the therapist is performing ego and superego functions by inhibiting destructive action and supporting the patient's weak superego by helping her to find alternatives to destructive behaviour.

Throughout the process it is essential that the link between the patient (or group) and the therapist is maintained because this link re-establishes the patient's hold on reality which in turn facilitates her developing observing ego. The patient needs to be aware that whatever is occurring in the course of her artistic expression is serving her own development. She is not merely acting out certain feelings which would prevent any growth. The original behaviours, such as bingeing and vomiting, are not repeated or reinforced or stimulated in the approach to the artwork. Instead, part of the energy that was endowed in them is used for a process which may prove to be transformative.

It is clear that many of these patients have great difficulty in symbolically transforming their intensely felt needs. Their abandonment of thinking and their reliance upon concrete expressions of their distress leads to further chaos in which they have little relationship with themselves and limited experience of themselves as inhabiting their own bodies.

The use of symbolic behaviour is a necessary development of the ego and enables the establishment of a defence against separation. In infancy, the internalization of the mother enables the infant to maintain the mother's image when she is absent. Without the capacity to experience symbols, the individual responds to images in a concrete fashion. The capacity to use symbols is dependent upon developing sufficient separateness between the self and the world, both externally and internally, that a bridging process becomes feasible. The symbolic function involves representation instead of identification. A patient who produces what appears to be powerful symbolic material may be unable to use it symbolically. In other words, there is a loss of the 'as if' quality of experience. This is demonstrated by a lack of the ability to abstract from the image. Although the therapist may view the content of the work as being symbolic, for the patient it may exist only as a feeling which changes from moment to moment.

Milner (1971) suggests that some drawings may not exhibit any recognizable comunication because certain ideas and feelings which are seeking expression have not yet been sufficiently worked over internally by the patient and so are not adequately sublimated. On the same subject Kramer (1977) states:

> Abandoning one's self to impulsive pleasures is intensely gratifying but the danger of excess and of the let-down that follows is every present . . . the pleasures of sublimation are more long lasting and often they are more exquisite, but they cannot be as intense. Sublimation depends on partial renunciation, for an instinct that spends itself through full gratification is not available as a source of energy for any modified activity.
>
> (Kramer 1977)

She goes on to explain that an instinct must have been sufficiently fulfilled when it originally appeared in order for it to be successfully modified. Otherwise, the instinctive need may remain overwhelming and obsessive. The therapeutic task is therefore to help the patient to transcend impulsive acting out and to progress to symbolic representational thought. To achieve this, the therapist must first join the patient at the more concrete level in order, through the art, to create the transitional bridges that can foster symbolization.

The difficulty in symbolic functioning appears not only in the content of the artwork but also in the patient's relationship to it. Robbins (1987) describes how

> Pathological solutions, such as splits, disparities in opposites, and the like will have aesthetic parallels in such areas as over-balances

in colour or shading, the expansion or contraction of space, rigidity of form and the flow and organization of energy.

(Robbins 1987)

He describes the way in which the art therapist is constantly engaged in attempting to relate aesthetics to developmental issues, so that the psychopathology of the patient can be directly worked with through the artistic medium. He declares:

Representations may be overly stilted and concrete, suggesting a rigid and/or narrow view of reality with an accompanying rigid defence system and ego structure. . . . as the patient gains more self-definition or structure and his observing ego develops, the art form produced likewise shows more definition and dimension- ality. Materials become the stuff with which the patients structure and share their perceptions and inner life – quite literally give them form.

(Robbins 1987)

The development of form within the artwork represents the patient's growing ability to differentiate objects from out of a background. The patient must be able to differentiate herself from other objects as well as to combine diverse and separate images of the self into one integrated representation. This work is not possible while the artwork comprises a sheet of paper which is totally covered with formless manifestations. As the patient develops an increased capacity for self-reflectiveness, so her thinking processes are utilized during the art therapy sessions.

A paradox arises when considering the patient who paints detailed, well-formed and perhaps artistically skilled images and yet who seems unable to relate to what she has created. In this case the art may serve as a façade behind which she consciously intends to keep her 'messy' side well hidden. She has no authentic relationship with the work and whatever she says about it appears merely intellectual and detached. The therapist has to find a way to engage with the genuine part of the patient or the artwork. This authenticity may be disguised by the patient's own articulacy or by the therapist's verbal interpretations. Many art therapists maintain that the therapeutic power lies in the actual process of making the artwork. The art can have an integrative function of its own. As the art activity involves sublimation of certain instincts which otherwise would demand full gratification, one can see how a certain degree of frustration must be tolerated by the patient. The art functions as a modified activity whereby the gratification has to be partially renounced. However, regressed work contains the spontaneous expression of impulses which are not always communicable and have not become sufficiently channelled. In order for a process of transformation to occur in the artwork itself and not simply as an expression of feelings, the therapist must be able to contain the patient's feelings, especially in the early stages when this is more important than offering interpretations. The colourful, formless pictures which so often present in the early stages of treatment depict no defined objects, no separate images contained within their own boundaried spaces and therefore no relationships between objects. It is the task of the therapist to facilitate these potential relationships between parts of the patient's picture, and so to help her to develop concepts of relatedness.

As the patient develops a more fully functioning autonomous self, she is also expanding her capacity to experience herself as more differentiated from significant others. This concerns her relationships not only with the real external people in her life but also within her own mind, those she enacts internally. By withdrawing some of the projections that she has made on to particular internal figures, she aids the process of becoming more separate from, say, her mother's attitude towards her. In time she may become more capable of distinguishing her mother's attitude from her own and so may increase the mental and bodily integration of her self.

The ability to experience a greater degree of separateness requires, amongst other things, an adaptive and healthy recognition of one's own aggression. A self-portrait depicting a little girl instead of a young woman serves to deny the patient's power, sexuality and aggression by portraying a fantasy, an idealized child. Since part of the constructive energy which goes into the making of art derives from neutralized aggression, adequate channels are needed in order to discharge these impulses. Certain images, such as wild animals in cages, convey a conscious awareness of the patient's fear of her own aggression; certain techniques, such as preparing clay or tearing magazines, require physical energy. The therapist's suggestions regarding the use of certain materials may coincide with the patient's developmental needs at a certain stage. Robbins (1987), a psychoanalyst and sculptor himself, discusses the ways in which a wide variety of art materials may be employed for patients at different stages. He relates how texture may be important in terms

of roughness or malleability and he considers the use of plaster, for
example, with its inherent transition from a warm, soft, flowing
liquid to cool, well-defined hardness. 'Its transitory nature might
be played with in instances where the issue of separation–individuation, involving the evolution of self–object differentiation and
definition, predominates' (Robbins 1987).

This highlights the importance of the art therapist's being alert to
the process involved in the artwork and to the therapeutic power
contained in the activity itself. The value of the process is clearly
demonstrated by Dalley (1987) when she talks of a patient's work:

> painting provided a means by which Henry could externalize his
> feelings and erode rigid defences. By continuing to express
> himself in this way, weakened, exposed boundaries could then
> be strengthened and consolidated. Through this, he could identify
> and resolve several conflicts that contributed to his breakdown.
>
> (Dalley, in Dalley *et al.* 1987)

Dalley describes how Henry, through channelling his aggression,
was able to become more aware of it as an emotion. By recognizing
one's emotions rather than playing them out through intellectual
pursuits, the individual is able to recognize the reality of his/her
internal world. This, in turn, enables a greater distinction to be made
between the internal and external worlds, between fantasy and
reality. The role of aggression is vital here. Dalley (1987) also
describes how an infant's destructive attacks on his/her objects
may be used as a constructive force to enable differentiation
between the self and object. When the infant comes to realize that
these fantasized attacks do not destroy the object in external reality,
it becomes possible to perceive the object as a separate and
independent entity, outside of the infant's omnipotent control.

This process is worked and reworked throughout the therapeutic
process. The relationship between these internal changes and the
artwork is understood by the art therapist who uses his/her famil-
iarity with the available materials to guide the patient appropriately.
Watercolours, which are difficult to control, require the painter to
work spontaneously and with a modicum of chance. Oils challenge
time and patience, and so test frustration tolerance. Working with
clay may arouse issues concerning early bowel control, mess,
expulsion, mastery and creation. With clay, the patient is immediately relating to three-dimensional space; mistakes can be repaired,
decisions can be reversed. Through the use of art there is a constant

exploration of not only form and shape but also issues relating to balance, cohesiveness and the framing of concepts. Art provides an extended language in which to work. Meaning is initially conveyed through concrete forms of communication. Images may be grounded or not, in the sense of depicting inner worlds of fantasy or reality; impoverished in their minimal content, pliable in their plasticity – they reflect a whole range of experiences which are visible rather than spoken. As Robbins (1987) cautions about spoken language, 'Words work along a continuum from concrete to abstract, directional or clarifying to symbolic or metaphorical. Higher levels of ego functioning are required for more meaningful abstract thinking and verbalization.'

This echoes the theme of the present book. There are many reasons why the more disturbed patient, especially one who mainly operates in a non-differentiated way, requires a relationship which is non-intrusive and 'felt' before she can make full use of words to help her to develop a separate self.

This is particularly important for these patients, so many of whom lack an authentic core. The establishment of a central core in the differentiation of a sense of self is one of the fundamental changes that can occur. Case and Dalley (1992) discuss Winnicott's ideas concerning the development of the true self. This occurs only when strength is given to the infant's weak ego by the mother's implementation of the infant's omnipotent expressions. 'A false self develops when a mother repeatedly fails to meet the infant's gesture and substitutes her own gesture. This is given sense by the compliance of the infant. The true self has spontaneity' (Case and Dalley 1992).

Although it must not be assumed that young adult patients are functioning as infants, there are some aspects of their development which may impede emotional growth. The art therapist must be open to these difficulties as they can be communicated through the art process and the images that are produced in therapy. In art therapy the need for spontaneity must be differentiated from impulsiveness. Spontaneous action carries with it a sense of mastery, of control. It allows freedom of expression to originate from the true part of the individual's self. It is not an enactment which is aimed at obliterating thought and feelings. The therapist must be aware, throughout the image-making process, of the patient's capacity to wipe out her thinking self or to become so immersed in the activity that she gives up her sense of self.

In the early stages of treatment or later, during regressive periods, a patient may paint without creating any links between either the images themselves or the images and herself. At other stages, the patient may use these fragments of images and thoughts and turn them into a more integrated entity.

The more disturbed the patient, the more evidence there is within the artwork, where images are attacked and destroyed or left incomplete or distorted. Spatial organization may be confused or the art may simply demonstrate a poverty of expression.

To be able to make symbolic use of the artwork, a patient must be able to experience simultaneously the concrete and the abstract, the known and the unknown, the 'I' and the 'not I'. A transitional object is considered to be an individual's early attempt at symbolizing, in order to create a bridge between the conscious and the unconscious. Prior to this stage, there is little experience either of differentiating the boundaries which define inside and outside or of 'I' and 'not I'. When the patient is predominantly functioning at this level, she thinks of two separate objects in such a way that the reality of one is denied, because it has been merged with the other. The work of the art therapist and others is to facilitate the patient's development beyond this level of functioning. This occurs, through the artwork, at a concrete level. The art therapist helps the patient slowly to disentangle the confused and combined images, creating the space for separate self and other images to exist. The fragile self, which is as yet undefined and has weak boundaries and which is disconnected from its own authentic core, is addressed again and again on a literal level through the imagery.

The capacity to symbolize represents the patient's development of a sense of separateness between herself and the world, both internally and externally, so that a bridging process becomes feasible. A pure 'action of feeling' expresses a state of fusion between the self and object, and the task of the therapist may then be to act primarily as a container. The therapist also may need to mediate the symbolic function for the patient by remaining aware of both the conscious and the unconscious elements of the patient's expression.

As mentioned earlier, an anorectic's self-portraits often demonstrate her conscious wish to be a young child. The desperate attempt to repudiate even the thought of having an adult female body is evident. Throughout treatment such images 'grow up' along with the artist, so that the ribbons and bows which so often accompanied the earlier pictures are replaced by more mature images. Not only the content of the images changes but also the style in which they are created. The patient in recovery may let go of her controllable felt-tip pens and experiment with watercolours, which allow for more spontaneity and less rigidity. Her stereotyped and repetitive drawings may give way to pictures which she risks creating on the spur of the moment. This marks a considerable change from the many months of sessions in which the patient created only pictures which she had planned in detail on the previous day.

An anorectic patient typically takes up little space on her paper. It is as though she does not feel entitled to possess the whole sheet. Both her low self-worth and the effort she expends on making herself appear unneedful are demonstrated in her art. As she progresses, these aspects change too; she may select better quality paper, her images may be more centrally placed and may become bolder and more assertive. The need to feel in control may give way to a greater spontaneity and flexibility, to a lessening of the orderly, often stereotyped symbols. Prior to this, the anorectic's self-esteem was maintained only by her ability to control her body.

A disturbed patient tends to be emotionally isolated, both within her social relationships and in relation to the external environment. She lives in a world where abstract ideas are manifested concretely. She struggles to create some semblance of order out of her inner turbulence, a sense of unity from her feelings of fragmentation. During treatment her sense of self begins to change. An individual identity, secure within the limits of her own body, takes shape. Reflected in the content of her artwork is her increasing ability to structure her impulses and aims in order to communicate with others. A more coherent form starts to emerge from the fragmented, incoherent images.

Case and Dalley (1992) describe a patient who took some clay and shaped it into a bowl. He then made a figure bending over the bowl as if vomiting into it. The 'vomit' was made of curled up tissue paper of different colours, with added paint to make a rich mixture. Another figure was made to one side, as if watching. The patient then moved the second figure to feed the first figure with a spoon from the bowl. The contents of the bowl had changed from 'vomit' to 'food'. The authors explain this process in the following way:

> In therapy it can feel as if one spews out angry, sad, difficult feelings in a jumble like vomit. These feelings need to be contained by the therapist within the room, the bowl. The

therapist needs to help the client re-incorporate these unwanted thoughts and feelings, the parts of ourselves we don't want or like, to understand them, the food.

(Case and Dalley 1992)

All therapeutic interventions should be aimed at facilitating the patient's dynamic progress from what may at first appear to be merely a static description of her mental state. A blank sheet of paper has been likened by McNeilly (1989) to the silences occurring in group psychotherapy which may be understood as items of communication. Recurring pictures may initially seem to be static and to have no quality of change but McNeilly links such repetitive patterns to Freud's 'compulsion to repeat' which is an ungovernable process originating in the unconscious (see Laplanche and Pontalis 1973). It often feels as if the repetition is a form of guarding against the distressing content that is being withheld. 'The hidden feeling behind the repeated image is a fear of change from the rigid and inferior presentation of the self' (McNeilly 1989). McNeilly also talks about the patient's need to copy pictures, in that 'a driving force may be that the copier may feel devoid or empty inside and they copy because they feel that they have little to give the world. There is a great ego deficiency here' (McNeilly 1989).

Thus, the therapist's capacity to help the patient to think about her work as a meaningful process and not as a static event brings about change in the individual. The patient becomes involved in an active process of development in which, for example, she begins to link fragmented concepts in her images into a more coherent entity.

The therapist may need to address the very process by which the patient makes her images. One patient, in her mid-twenties, typically sped through the allocated time for painting in just a few minutes and would then distract herself whilst waiting for the rest of the group to complete their work. With the therapist's help she came to understand this behaviour and to appreciate how incapable she felt of staying with any painful image for more than a few seconds and so would literally run away from her own awareness. For her, change involved both slowing down her pace and having the support that enabled her to begin to tolerate her own thoughts and feelings which were created by her artwork. Another change which she made after some time was to allow her self-images to grow up slowly. In the early stages, she had persistently portrayed herself as a small child in relation to fully grown adults. Over time, her perception of herself and of others became more realistic, and so the images that she drew changed accordingly. The art therapist must be aware of the patient's capacity to experience certain emotional states. As Robbins (1987) explains, 'Growth occurs from the process of going through the pain of an unmet stage of development rather than from the therapist's gratifying the patient's hunger.' However, this does not mean that the therapist withholds helpful interventions which may facilitate the patient's grasp on reality. Kramer describes a child, waiting to be given his paint tray, who screamed, 'I have no paint, I have no paint. Who stole my paint?' She intervened with: 'Why do you have no paint? Who is giving out the paint? How many trays are left for Tommy to hand out?' In other words, she led him towards a realistic understanding of the situation that he had interpreted in a paranoid manner. This example demonstrates the way in which the art therapist may intervene in order to recapture reality.

Patients with eating disorders lack the ability to regulate themselves internally. They have no secure internal reference point. They use food as the most basic external means to try to compensate for this deficiency, to try to heal their poor mind/body integration. In an attempt to increase their sense of bodily integration, they may resort to a variety of self-stimulating behaviours, ranging from self-mutilation to the wearing of tight clothes which reinforce the body-edge. These behaviours counteract the patients' dreaded states of emptiness or deadness.

Much of this book has been concerned with how art therapists can facilitate these patients' awareness of their core self, which can then be related authentically to another, in what may be termed symbolic exchange relationships. Projection and projective identification mark the beginnings of an exchange between subject and object. The infant projects unwanted parts of him/herself into the mother for her to hold for him/her and to feed back later in a safely digested form. If the mother is unable to do this sufficiently, she may see only what she has projected into her infant. At these and later stages, thought and symbolic communication can occur without language. Indeed, vision plays a significant role in the formation of unconscious symbols, whereas language is thought to be auditory–vocal in origin. Thus, whatever is visible through the medium of art communicates vital information and serves to facilitate the development of symbolic capacities.

Just as the obese person has, in a literal and concrete way, become enveloped with protective layers, so the images of these patients often convey a similar process. The protective layers may be represented in a variety of ways, through which may be understood the patients' defensive need to draw back their ego into the core of their self. Figure 10.1 depicts the extra emphasis that a patient placed around the outline of her body in order to protect herself against the invading arrows. She talked about her fear of anyone getting too close to her and of her need to keep them at bay. However, she felt helpless in the face of others' demands on her. This sense of powerlessness was conveyed in the drawing by her lack of arms. Her lack of assertiveness meant that she could not set appropriate boundaries for herself and therefore, as a form of self-protection, she relied upon isolating herself and rejecting people.

The growth of the distinction between the self and another occurs as a result of the gradual transition from predominantly narcissistic functioning to the individual's recognition of others as separate to herself. The ego becomes confined within the body. The skin surface is tremendously important in aiding this by, in effect, providing a

Figure 10.1

sensation ego to be used for either positive (e.g. touch) or negative (e.g. self-mutilation) experiences.

The tendency towards self-destructive behaviour is a major feature of borderline conditions. Some patients describe being pulled back again and again into their own tortuous prison even when they see a door left open for them. The behaviour itself comprises an addiction which must be compulsively repeated. Joseph (1982) describes patients who are in this state as being 'enthralled' by their destructive drive, as if it contained a romantic or sexual element. Thus, the pull on these patients may contain an element of sado-masochism. The sadistic part of the self relentlessly attacks the other part. Understanding the secret and violent internal world of these patients is an essential part of the therapist's ability to help them. The extent of these patients' self-abuse, which is demonstrated in a wide range of bodily attacks, may in part be the result of their identifying their own bodies with parts of the hated object. For those patients who have been the passive recipient of painful experiences, the situation is now reversed and they become their own torturer. They are now, at least in fantasy, in a position of control.

This book has explored the relationship of these patients with the various parts of themselves and the consequent implications for their relationships with others. One of the recurring themes has been the problem of separation and dependency: the conflicting need for separateness and for relatedness, for belonging and for individuation. The boundary of the patient must be neither too permeable nor too impermeable. The former leads to fragmentation and symbiosis, the latter to isolation. Both lead to loss of self.

The symbiotically attached person cannot manage the experience of dependency because she does not have a clear delineation between herself and the other person. She seeks some form of defence in order to protect herself against recognizing her separateness, since this would result in her having to experience her dependency on others. She therefore experiences a range of disruptive feelings such as envy, when recognizing the other's good qualities, or frustration, in response to wishes not being met. She has many cannibalistic fantasies and she makes desperate attempts to achieve magical control over her own body and that of others.

Part of the reason behind the patient's narcissistic form of object-relating is therefore to deny separateness and to attempt to remain in an omnipotent world of magical control where she is relating to parts of the self, which are located in others through the process of projective identification, rather than to actual separate objects. To relinquish such magical control means that the patient is confronted by the strength of her destructive and envious impulses, which she then has to manage.

Of course there are parts of the patient which are not in collusion with her self-destructive forces and it is vital that the therapist recognizes these healthy and creative aspects and encourages their growth by using techniques which encourage play, spontaneity and enjoyment. The therapeutic process is not only about tolerating pain but also about the ability to celebrate living.

References

Abraham, K. (1979) *Selected Papers on Psycho-Analysis*, London: Karnac Books Ltd.

Arieti, S. (1976) *Creativity: The Magic Synthesis*, New York: Basic Books.

Atwood, M. (1980) *The Edible Woman*, London: Virago Press.

—— (1982) *Lady Oracle*, London, Virago Press.

Bick, E. (1968) 'The experience of the skin in early object relations', *International Journal of Psychoanalysis* 49.

Boris, H. N. (1984) 'On the treatment of anorexia nervosa', *International Journal of Psychoanalysis* 65 (4).

Brown, L. J. (1985) 'On concreteness', *The Psychoanalytic Review* 72 (3).

Brown, N. O. (1959) *Life against Death: The Psychoanalytical Meaning of History*, Middletown, Conn.: Wesleyan University Press.

Bruch, H. (1974) *Eating Disorders, Obesity, Anorexia Nervosa and the Person Within*, London: Routledge & Kegan Paul.

Campbell, J. (1929) *Primitive Mythology: The Masks of God*, New York: Penguin Books.

Case, C. and Dalley, T. (1992) *The Handbook of Art Therapy*, London and New York: Tavistock/Routledge.

Chernin, K. (1983) *Woman Size*, London: The Women's Press.

Conrad, P. (1986) *Sunday Observer Magazine*, 22 June

Dalley, T., Case, C., Shaverien, J., Weir, F., Halliday, D., Nowellhall, L. and Waller, D. (1987) *Images of Art Therapy: New Developments in Theory and Practice*, London and New York: Tavistock.

Davidson, A. and Fay, J. (1972) *Fantasy in Childhood*, Westport, Conn.: Greenwood Press.

Davis, M. and Wallbridge, D. (1981) *Boundary and Space*, London: Karnac Books.

Douglas, M. (1966) *Purity and Danger*, London: Routledge & Kegan Paul.

—— (1973) *Natural Symbols*, London: Barrie & Jenkins.

Evans-Pritchard, E. (1976) *Witchcraft, Oracles and Magic Among the Azande*, Oxford: Oxford University Press.

Fairbairn, W. R. D. (1952) *Psycho-Analytic Studies of the Personality*, London: Tavistock.

Fenichel, O. (1946) *The Psychoanalytic Theory of Neurosis*, London: Routledge & Kegan Paul.

Frazer, J. G. (1957) *The Golden Bough: A Study in Magic and Religion*, (abridged edn), London: Macmillan.

Freud, S. (1960) *Totem and Taboo*, London: Routledge & Kegan Paul.

———— (1964) *Moses and Monotheism: An Outline of Psycho-Analysis and Other Works*, London: Hogarth Press.

———— (1985) *Civilisation and its Discontents and Other Works*, London: Penguin.

Gilroy, A. and Dalley, T. (eds) (1989) *Pictures at an Exhibition: Selected Essays on Art and Art Therapy*, London and New York: Tavistock/ Routledge.

Goldstein, W. (1985) *An Introduction to the Borderline Conditions*, Northvale, NJ and London: Jason Aronson.

Goodsitt, A. (1985) 'Self psychology and the treatment of anorexia nervosa', in D. Garner and P. Garfinkel (eds), *The Handbook of Psychotherapy for Anorexia Nervosa and Bulimia*, New York and London: Guilford Press.

Guntrip, H. (1982) *Personality Structure and Human Interaction*, International Psycho-Analytic Library 56, London: Hogarth Press.

Joseph, B. (1982) 'Addiction to near-death', *International Journal of Psychoanalysis* 63.

Kestenberg, J. (1956) 'Vicissitudes of female sexuality', *Journal of the American Psychoanalytic Association*, 11.

Klein, M. (1961a) *Love, Guilt and Reparation and Other Works 1921–45*, London: Hogarth Press.

———— (1961b) *Envy and Gratitude and Other Works 1946–63*, London: Hogarth Press.

Kramer, E. (1977) *Art as Therapy with Children*, New York: Schocken Books.

Krueger, D. W. (1989) *Body Self and Psychological Self*, New York: Brunner/Mazel.

Laing, R. D. (1960) *The Divided Self*, London: Tavistock.

———— (1970) *The Predicament of the Family*, New York: International Universities Press.

Laplanche, J., Pontalis, J. B. and Khan, R. (1983) *The Language of Psycho-Analysis*, (2nd edn), London: Hogarth Press.

Little, M. (1985) *Winnicott Working in Areas where Psychotic Anxieties Predominate*, Free Association 3, London: Free Association Books.

McNeilly, G. (1989) 'Group analytic art groups', in A. Gilroy and T. Dalley (eds), *Pictures at an Exhibition: Selected Essays on Art and Art Therapy*, London: Tavistock/Routledge.

Meyer, B. C. and Weinroth, L. A. (1957) 'Observations on Psychological Aspects of Anorexia Nervosa', *Psychosomatic Medicine* 19.

Milner, M. (1952) 'Aspects of symbolism in comprehension of the not-self', *International Journal of Psychoanalysis* 33.

———— (1971) *On not Being Able to Paint*, London: Heinemann.

Modell, A. H. (1969) *Object Love and Reality*, International Psycho-Analytic Library 78, London: Hogarth Press.

Pankow, G. (1976) 'Dynamic structurisation in schizophrenia', in A. Burton (ed.), *Psychotherapy of the Psychoses*, New York: Basic Books.

———— (1981) 'Psychotherapy, a psychoanalytic approach: An analytic approach employing the concepts of the "body image" ', in M. Dongier and E. D. Wittkower (eds), *Divergent Views in Psychiatry*, Cambridge and London: Harper & Row.

Peto, A. (1959) 'Body image and archaic thinking', *International Journal of Psychoanalysis* 40.

Piaget, J. (1929) *The Child's Conception of the World*, London: Routledge & Kegan Paul.

Pickford, R. W. (1967) *Studies in Psychiatric Art*, Springfield, Ill.: Charles C. Thomas.

Plath, S. (1963) 'Ocean 1212', *The Listener*, 29 August.

Prestage, R. O. (1976) 'Anorexia nervosa as a stage of recovery in the treatment of an adolescent girl', *Journal of Child Psychotherapy* 4 (2).

Raphael-Leff, J. (1986) *Vogue*, June.

Robbins, A. (1987) *The Artist as Therapist*, New York: Human Sciences Press.

Rose, G. J. (1963) 'Body ego and creative imagination', *Journal of the American Psychoanalytical Association* 11.

———— (1964) 'Creative imagination in terms of ego core and boundaries', *Journal of Psychoanalysis* 45.

Rosen, J. and Leitenberg, H. (1985) 'Exposure plus response prevention treatment of bulimia', in D. Garner and P. Garfinkel (eds), *The Handbook of Psychotherapy for Anorexia Nervosa and Bulimia*, New York and London: Guilford Press.

Rycroft, C. (1968) *A Critical Dictionary of Psychoanalysis*, London: Penguin.

Selvini Palazzoli, M. (1974) *Self Starvation*, Sussex: Chaucer Publishing.

Schilder, P. (1970) *The Image and Appearance of the Human Body*, New York: International Universities Press.

Sours, J. (1980) *Starving to Death in a Sea of Objects: The Anorexia Nervosa Syndrome*, New York: Jason Aronson.

Sprince, M. P. (1984) 'Early psychic disturbances in anorectic and bulimic patients as reflected in the psychoanalytic process', *Journal of Child Psychotherapy* 10 (2).

Thevoz, M. (1984) *The Painted Body*, New York: Rizzoli International Publishing Inc.

Winnicott, D. W. (1980) *Playing and Reality*, London: Penguin.

Index